Congressional
Research
Service

U.S. Wind Turbine Manufacturing:
Federal Support for an Emerging Industry

Michaela D. Platzer
Specialist in Industrial Organization and Business

December 18, 2012

Congressional Research Service

7-5700

www.crs.gov

R42023

CRS Report for Congress ——————————————————

Prepared for Members and Committees of Congress

Summary

Increasing U.S. energy supply diversity has been the goal of many Presidents and Congresses. This commitment has been prompted by concerns about national security, the environment, and the U.S. balance of payments. Investments in new energy sources also have been seen as a way to expand domestic manufacturing. For all of these reasons, the federal government has a variety of policies to promote wind power.

Expanding the use of wind energy requires installation of wind turbines. These are complex machines composed of some 8,000 components, created from basic industrial materials such as steel, aluminum, concrete, and fiberglass. Major components in a wind turbine include the rotor blades, a nacelle and controls (the heart and brain of a wind turbine), a tower, and other parts such as large bearings, transformers, gearboxes, and generators. Turbine manufacturing involves an extensive supply chain. Until recently, Europe has been the hub for turbine production, supported by national renewable energy deployment policies in countries such as Denmark, Germany, and Spain. However, support for renewable energy including wind power has begun to wane across Europe as governments there reduce or remove some subsidies. Competitive wind turbine manufacturing sectors are also located in India and Japan and are emerging in China and South Korea.

U.S. and foreign manufacturers have expanded their capacity in the United States to assemble and produce wind turbines and components. About 470 U.S. manufacturing facilities produced wind turbines and components in 2011, up from as few as 30 in 2004. An estimated 30,000 U.S. workers were employed in the manufacturing of wind turbines in 2011. Because turbine blades, towers, and certain other components are large and difficult to transport, manufacturing clusters have developed in certain states, notably Colorado, Iowa, and Texas, which offer proximity to the best locations for wind energy production. The U.S. wind turbine manufacturing industry also depends on imports, with the majority coming from European countries, where the technical ability to produce large wind turbines was developed. Although turbine manufacturers' supply chains are global, recent investments are estimated to have raised the share of parts manufactured in the United States to 67% in 2011, up from 35% in 2005-2006.

The outlook for wind turbine manufacturing in the United States is more uncertain now than in recent years. For the past two decades, a variety of federal laws and state policies have encouraged both wind energy production and the use of U.S.-made equipment to generate that energy. One apparent challenge for the industry is the scheduled expiration at year-end 2012 of the production tax credit (PTC), which the industry claims could reduce domestic turbine sales to zero in 2013. In anticipation, at least a dozen wind turbine manufacturers announced layoffs or hiring freezes at their U.S. facilities in 2012, citing uncertainty around the renewal of the PTC as one reason. Other factors affecting the health of the U.S. wind industry are intense price competition from natural gas, an oversupply in wind turbines, and softening demand for renewable electricity.

Contents

Figures

Tables

Appendixes

Contacts

Introduction

This report discusses the U.S. wind turbine manufacturing industry, its supply chain, employment and international trade trends, major federal policy efforts aimed at supporting the industry, and issues affecting its future. The wind industry's national trade group, the American Wind Energy Association (AWEA), reported an estimated 30,000 Americans were employed directly and indirectly in wind turbine manufacturing in 2011, compared to 2,500 in 2004. Another 45,000 U.S. workers reportedly were employed in other parts of the wind industry in 2011, including construction and services.[1] Wind turbine equipment and component manufacturing jobs range in pay from about $30,000 to around $90,000, according to the Bureau of Labor Statistics.[2] Following an unprecedented period of growth in the U.S. wind power market between 2005 and 2009, about half as many new wind turbines were installed in 2011 (some 3,500) as in 2009.

Aside from GE Energy and Clipper Windpower, most of the manufacturers that sell, assemble, or manufacture turbines and wind-related components in the U.S. market are headquartered outside the United States. Vestas, Gamesa, and Siemens are among the European manufacturers that have responded to government regulations that mandate the use of renewables, including wind power. Other firms manufacturing wind turbines for the U.S. wind market include Japanese and Indian companies such as Mitsubishi and Suzlon. Manufacturers from South Korea and China are also expanding production capacity and entering the U.S. market.

Federal interest in the U.S. wind turbine manufacturing industry is based on (1) increasing the role of clean energy technology in energy production; (2) encouraging advanced manufacturing and the creation of skilled manufacturing jobs; and (3) enhancing the diversity of U.S. energy sources.[3]

Wind energy, like many energy technologies, benefits from government incentives.[4] Without them, it does not appear likely that there would be a U.S. wind turbine industry. To a large extent, the federal government sets the framework and influences the pace of domestic wind power development.

One of the main federal policy tools to encourage wind generation is a tax credit, known as the production tax credit (PTC), which is slated to expire at the end of 2012.[5] Other policy drivers include state renewable portfolio standards, which have been adopted by more than half the states to mandate production of electricity from "clean" sources.[6] No nationwide renewable electricity

---

[1] Employment data for the U.S. wind energy sector is currently only reported by the American Wind Energy Association (AWEA). Recent statistics can be found in AWEA's annual report, *U.S. Wind Industry Annual Market Report Year Ending 2011*, p. 49.

[2] BLS does not publish earnings data specific to the wind power industry, but it estimates that earnings for engineers in wind power are comparable to earnings for engineers in general. James Hamilton and Drew Liming, *Careers in Wind Energy*, Bureau of Labor Statistics, September 2010, pp. 10-11, http://www.bls.gov/green/wind_energy/wind_energy.pdf.

[3] The U.S. Energy Information Administration (EIA) reports wind energy represented about 4% of U.S. power generating capacity, and 3% of total U.S. electricity generation in 2011.

[4] EIA, *Direct Federal Financial Interventions and Subsidies in Energy in Fiscal Year 2010*, July 2011, http://docs.wind-watch.org/US-subsidy-2010.pdf.

[5] For a detailed discussion on energy tax incentives see CRS Report R41953, *Energy Tax Incentives: Measuring Value Across Different Types of Energy Resources*, by Molly F. Sherlock.

[6] EIA, Renewable and Alternative Fuels, *Renewable Portfolio Standards and State Mandates by State*, August 2011, (continued...)

---

standard currently exists, but the Obama Administration and some Members of Congress have endorsed the concept.[7] These policies do not directly address manufacturing, but greater wind power adoption supports the development of a U.S. wind energy manufacturing base. In addition, the federal government and some state governments have maintained programs that provide financial incentives for manufacturing of wind power equipment.

Many international wind turbine manufacturers and component suppliers have opened manufacturing facilities in the United States since 2005. In 2011, there were more than 470 U.S.-based wind turbine manufacturing facilities—a 10-fold increase in five years—ranging from wind turbine assembly plants to factories producing various wind-related components including large bearings, castings, electrical wiring, fasteners, hydraulics, and power electronics. Only a small number of these factories are dedicated exclusively to building turbine parts (blades, towers, and nacelles); the others manufacture components for various industrial uses, including wind-specific products. Given the interest in wind power around the world, manufacturers with U.S. production facilities may be able to increase exports of advanced wind-energy components. Around $250 million in fully assembled wind turbines were exported from the United States in 2011.

The industry's future in the absence of government support, however, is open to question. While the cost of electricity from land-based wind turbines is less than the cost of power from other alternative sources, such as concentrated solar plants and geothermal installations, it is still, in general, somewhat higher than the cost of power from new gas-fired generators. This means that without government support, electricity suppliers' demand for wind turbines would be relatively limited. It is possible that, if existing policy tools are allowed to expire, wind industry manufacturing will face a difficult future. On the other hand, it is imaginable that technological improvements in wind generation and higher costs for construction of fossil-fuel power plants could at some point make wind cost-competitive with coal and gas as a source of electricity, creating a brighter outlook for wind turbine manufacturing.

Wind Turbine Manufacturing

Wind turbine manufacturing is at the core of the multifaceted wind power industry. Because of the use of castings, forgings, and machining, turbine manufacturing is a significant contributor to U.S. heavy manufacturing. By the end of 2011, more than 38,000 wind turbines were installed in the United States.[8] Procurement of wind turbines accounts for an estimated 60% to 70% of overall expenses for wind energy developers.[9]

The market potential of offshore wind power is not covered in this report. No offshore projects have been installed in the United States to date, and the industry faces difficulties with permitting, financing, and infrastructure availability.[10] So far, Cape Wind, off the coast of Nantucket in

---

(...continued)

http://www.eia.gov/cneaf/solar.renewables/page/trends/table28.html.

[7] The Clean Energy Standard Framework announced by the White House in 2011 is discussed in CRS Report, R41720, *Clean Energy Standard: Design Elements, State Baseline Compliance and Policy Considerations*, by Phillip Brown.

[8] AWEA, U.S. Wind Industry Annual Market Report 2011, p. 40.

[9] Worldwatch Institute, *Made in China, or Made by China? Chinese Wind Turbine Manufacturers Struggle to Enter Own Market*, http://www.worldwatch.org/node/3931.

[10] U.S. Department of Energy, *A National Offshore Wind Strategy: Creating an Offshore Wind Energy Industry in the* (continued...)

Massachusetts, is the only project that has a commercial wind energy development lease with the U.S. government. AWEA reports that at the end of 2011, there were 15 different proposed offshore wind projects in the United States, and a proposed offshore transmission line.[11] Also, this report does not cover small wind turbine manufacturing, which AWEA defines as turbines with rated capacities of 100 kilowatts (kW) or less. This segment of the wind turbine market appears to be growing. According to the World Wind Energy Association, worldwide more than 330 manufacturers offer small wind turbines.[12] AWEA's most recent data indicate that 95 manufacturers of small wind turbines were based in the United States in 2009.[13]

Historical Overview

The use of a wind turbine to generate electricity is an American invention of the late 19th century.[14] The development of U.S. commercial wind turbine manufacturing can be traced back to the 1970s, when the U.S. government advanced the technology in response to the oil crises of 1973 and 1979 as an alternative to power generation from fossil fuels.

The first U.S. wind farms were developed in California, an early adopter of policies favorable to wind energy, and the state dominated worldwide wind development in the early 1980s.[15] This created a market for wind turbine manufacturers. Enertech, U.S. Windpower (renamed Kenetech in 1988), and Zond were among the American suppliers. Other U.S. manufacturers included technology and aerospace firms such as Westinghouse and Boeing. In 1986, 60 U.S. firms produced turbines for the California market.[16] Foreign suppliers from Denmark, Germany, Japan, and the Netherlands, among other countries, also sold their wind turbines in California.[17] The California "wind rush" became the training ground for several firms, including the Danish manufacturer Vestas, now the world's largest manufacturer of utility-scale wind turbines.[18]

(...continued)

United States, February 2011, http://www1.eere.energy.gov/windandhydro/pdfs/national_offshore_wind_strategy.pdf.

[11] AWEA, U.S. Wind Industry Annual Market Report 2011, p. 57.

[12] AWEA, *2011 U.S. Small Wind Turbine Market Report*, June 2012, p. 22, http://www.awea.org/learnabout/smallwind/upload/AWEA_SmallWindReport-YE-2011.pdf.

[13] AWEA, *2010 Small Wind Turbine Global Market Study*, Year Ending 2009, p. 18, http://www.awea.org/learnabout/smallwind/upload/2010_AWEA_Small_Wind_Turbine_Global_Market_Study.pdf.

[14] Charles F. Brush, an American inventor, constructed the first modern wind turbine in 1888, in Cleveland, OH, for the purpose of electricity generation. He used it to power his home. Thereafter, other Americans such as Palmer C. Putman built wind turbine generators, mostly for farm use, at a time when electricity distribution systems had not yet been installed. U.S. manufacturers of early wind turbine generators included Jacobs Wind and Parris-Dunn. The rural electrification project of 1936 effectively killed the wind-generated power market in the United States until the early 1970s. For more information, see Windsector, *The First Wind Turbine in the United States*, April 17, 2011, http://windsector.tumblr.com/post/4711554356/the-first-wind-turbine-in-america.

[15] Janet Swain, "The Role of Government in the Development and Diffusion of Renewable Energy Technologies: Wind Power in the United States, California, Denmark, and Germany," (Ph.D. dissertation, Fletcher School of Law and Diplomacy, 2001), pp. 200-203. This dissertation notes that by 1991 77% of the world's wind capacity was installed in California.

[16] Geoffrey Jones and Loubna Bouamane, "Historical Trajectories and Corporate Competences in Wind Energy," (Working Paper 11-112, Harvard Business School, 2011), p. 32. http://www.hbs.edu/research/pdf/11-112.pdf.

[17] Over 15,000 medium-sized wind turbines were installed in California between 1981 and 1986. See Union of Concerned Scientists, Briefing on How Wind Energy Works, http://www.ucsusa.org/clean_energy/coalvswind/brief_wind.html.

[18] Large wind turbines are often called utility-scale because they generate enough power for utilities, or electric (continued...)

However, a drop in oil prices, along with reductions in government tax credits, caused a near total collapse of this market in the mid-1980s.[19] By the end of the decade, many wind turbine manufacturers went bankrupt as the industry adjusted to a much smaller market.

For the next two decades fuel prices were low and U.S. incentives spotty. In the United States, annual installed wind power capacity slowed from 1987 to 2000. The entire U.S. wind fleet exceeded 1,000 megawatts (MW) for the first time in 1986, but then took 13 years to reach approximately 2,400 MW.[20]

In the 1990s a more sustained market for wind power and wind turbine manufacturing evolved overseas. Strong, consistent government incentives and policies, which have included a policy mix of direct government investment, tax breaks, loans, regulations and laws that cap or tax emissions, supported the development of manufacturers abroad, particularly in Europe.[21] This allowed wind turbine manufacturers to establish themselves in countries such as Denmark, Spain, and Germany, where many wind turbine manufacturers are now based.[22]

Demand for Wind Turbines and Components

Demand for wind turbines and components is driven by growth in wind power capacity. More consistent U.S. policies have resulted in a substantial increase in cumulative utility-scale wind power capacity, from 9,000 MW in 2005 to more than 46,000 MW in 2011.[23] The United States was second to China in cumulative and new installed wind power capacity in 2011.[24] China and the United States accounted for more than 45% of total installed worldwide wind power capacity at the end of 2011.[25] The size of the U.S. market has made the United States an attractive

---

(...continued)

companies, to sell.

[19] Jens Vestergaard, Lotte Brandstrup, and Robert Goddard, *Industry Formation and State Intervention: The Case of the Wind Turbine Industry in Denmark and the United States*, Published in the Academy of International Business Conference Proceedings, p. 16-18, http://pure.au.dk/portal/files/2552/windmill_paper2.pdf.

[20] Lester Brown, *World on the Edge: How to Prevent Environmental and Economic Collapse*, Earth Policy Institute, Supporting Data Showing Cumulative Installed Wind Power Capacity and Annual Additions to the United States, 1980-2009, 2011, http://www.earth-policy.org/books/wote/wote_data_topic.

[21] An overview of policy instruments used by various governments to promote renewables, including wind power, can be found on the Renewable Energy Policy Network website at http://www.ren21.net/RenewablesPolicy/PolicyInstruments/tabid/5608/Default.aspx.

[22] The wind turbine industry advanced in Europe, specifically in Denmark, beginning in the early 20th century based largely on the wind turbines constructed by Poul la Cour. For background, see Jens Vestergaard, Lotte Brandstrup, and Robert Goddard, *"A Brief History of the Wind Turbine Industries in Denmark and the United States,"* (Academy of International Business, 2004), http://www.hha.dk/man/cmsdocs/publications/windmill_paper1.pdf.

[23] AWEA, *U.S. Wind Industry Annual Market Report 2011*, p. 4. Utility-scale wind turbines as defined by AWEA are large turbines with generating capacity of 100 kW and larger.

[24] China faces major challenges with grid connection of installed wind turbines, as some projects in China have to wait several months before being connected to the national grid. Thus, the United States continues to exceed China in grid connected wind power capacity. China issues two figures when it reports its wind power data. By year-end 2011, China reported that it installed 62.4 gigawatts (GW) of onshore wind power, but only 45 GW was operational and connected to the grid. In other markets, it is common practice to count all turbines as soon as they are grid connected and producing electricity. For more information see REN21, *Renewables 2011 Global Status Report*, Table R8, p. 104, http://www.ren21.net/Portals/97/documents/GSR/GSR2012_low%20res_FINAL.pdf.

[25] Global Wind Energy Council (GWEC) *Global Wind 2011 Report*, March 2012, p. 11, http://www.gwec.net/fileadmin/documents/Publications/Global_Wind_2007_report/
(continued...)

---

investment location for wind turbine and wind component manufacturers. However, the prospects for 2013 and beyond are clouded owing to several factors, including the fate of the PTC, low-cost natural gas, and manufacturing overcapacity in the wind turbine sector.[26]

Major customers for wind turbine manufacturers are large independent power producers (IPPs) and utilities such as Iberdrola Renewables, NextEra Energy Resources, Horizon-EDPR, Terra-Gen, Duke Energy, or Xcel Energy, which purchase wind turbines for commercial electricity generation.[27] Other wind turbine customers include universities and military bases, but these customers account for a very small share of the market.

Commercial utility-scale onshore wind turbines are installed at wind farms, which are clusters of wind turbines grouped together to produce large amounts of electricity. Currently, there are some 975 wind farms in the United States.[28] The largest is located in California, and there are several huge wind farms in Texas (see **Table 1**), which is by far the leading state in wind energy output, with over 10,000 MW of installed capacity at year-end 2011. Other large wind-power projects are in Indiana, Oregon, and Iowa. Several large U.S. wind farms are owned and managed by overseas companies. For example, the Roscoe, TX, wind farm is owned and operated by Germany-based E.ON Climate and Renewables. It consists of more than 600 wind turbines purchased from three different manufacturers: Mitsubishi, General Electric (GE), and Siemens.

Table 1. Largest U.S. Wind Power Projects

Project Name	State	Installed Capacity (MW)	Year Online	Owner	Number of Turbines/Manufacturer(s)
Alta Wind Project	California	981.0	2010, 2011	Terra-Gen Power	377/Vestas
Roscoe	Texas	781.5	2008	E.On Climate & Renewables	627/Mitsubishi, Siemens, GE
Horse Hollow	Texas	735.5	2006, 2006	NextEra Energy Resources	421,GE/Siemens
Capricorn Ridge	Texas	662.5	2007, 2008	NextEra Energy Resources	407,Mitsubishi/Siemens
Sweetwater	Texas	585.3	2003, 2005, 2007	Babcock & Brown Wind, Catamount	392/Vestas,GE/Siemens

Source: American Wind Energy Association (AWEA), U.S. Wind Industry Annual Market Report, 2011, p. 32.

(...continued)

GWEC%20Global%20Wind%20Report%202010%20low%20res.pdf.

[26] Ryan Wiser and Mark Bolinger, *2011 Wind Technologies Market Report*, Lawrence Berkeley National Laboratory, August 2012, p. 19, http://www1.eere.energy.gov/wind/pdfs/2011_wind_technologies_market_report.pdf.

[27] Independent power producers are companies that produce power that they sell to electric utilities.

[28] A list of some 975 wind farms in the United States can be accessed at Windpower's wind turbine and wind farms database, http://www.thewindpower.net/country-datasheet-windfarms-4-usa.php.

Wind Turbine Suppliers

International Manufacturers Dominate Wind Turbine Manufacturing

In 2011, 10 wind turbine manufacturers accounted for 85% of the global market measured by newly installed capacity. The three largest manufacturers were:

- Vestas at 12.9% (Denmark);

- Goldwind at 9.4% (China); and

- GE at 8.8% (U.S.).[29]

Other leading manufacturers are listed in **Appendix A**. These firms are headquartered in Europe, the United States, India, and China. GE Energy[30] and UTC/Clipper Windpower[31] are the only U.S.-headquartered utility-scale wind turbine manufacturers.

Some manufacturers, including Gamesa, Vestas, and Suzlon, focus exclusively on wind turbines. Others are part of larger diversified companies. All pursue a global business strategy, which means selling outside their home markets. Many operate manufacturing facilities throughout the world, including the United States, Europe, and China.

Recently, several Chinese companies have begun producing wind turbines, selling mainly in the large and growing China market.[32] China, which had virtually no wind turbine manufacturing capabilities in 2005, is now home to over 270 producers,[33] some of them capable of producing complete wind turbine systems with locally made products.[34] Four of the top 10 manufacturers worldwide in 2011 were headquartered in China (see **Appendix A**), where, by some estimates, turbines can be manufactured for 30% less than in Europe, the United States, or Japan.[35] Some Chinese firms apparently are looking for overseas markets,[36] but concerns about the quality of

---

[29] Ekopolitan, "World Turbine Market Shares, 2008-2011, Installed Capacity" BTM Estimates, http://www.ekopolitan.com/tech/global-wind-turbine-market-shares.

[30] Zond was purchased by Enron Wind in 1997. In 2002, GE, which had long produced turbines for power generation, acquired Enron Wind's fully integrated wind power capacity including its line of wind turbine generators.

[31] Clipper Windpower does not rank among the top 10 global wind turbine manufacturers and it has found itself squeezed in the United States, its main market, by larger competitors. In December 2010, United Technologies Corporation purchased Clipper, which it sold in August 2012 to a private equity firm, Platinum Equity. Clipper has downsized its operations and reduced its staff to fewer than 100 employees.

[32] GWEC reports China's wind market doubled every year between 2006 and 2009, and it has been the largest annual market by installed capacity in the world since 2009. GWEC, *Global Wind 2011 Report*, March 2012, p. 12, http://gwec.net/wp-content/uploads/2012/06/Annual_report_2011_lowres.pdf.

[33] Joshua Meltzer, *The United States and China: The Next Five Years*, The Brookings Institution, May 19, 2011, p. 17, http://www.brookings.edu/~/media/Files/events/2011/0519_us_china/20110519_us_china_panel4.pdf.

[34] Geoffrey Jones and Loubna Bouamane, *Historical Trajectories and Corporate Competences in Wind Energy*, (Working Paper 11-112, Harvard Business School, 2011), p. 55.

[35] Joanna Lewis, *Why China is acting on Clean Energy: Successes, Challenges, and Implications*, Georgetown University, October 12, 2012, p. 12, http://files.eesi.org/Lewis101212.pdf.

[36] John McDonald, *Wind Power Market Opportunity Profile, China*, British Columbia Trade and Investment, 2009, pp. 2-3, https://trade.britishcolumbia.ca/Export/Markets/Documents/China_WindPower.pdf.

Chinese turbines are one factor that might limit foreign sales since Chinese-made turbines are not yet seen as being as high in quality as European and American ones.[37]

South Korean companies are also making huge investments in wind turbine production. Two large South Korean shipbuilders, Hyundai Heavy Industries and Samsung Heavy Industries, have announced their intention to manufacture wind turbines. Other Korean firms undertaking wind turbine technology development include Daewoo, Hanjin, STX, Rotem, and Unisom. Additionally, South Korean wind turbine component manufacturers like Doosan, Hanjin, Taewoong, Hyosung, CS Wind, and Korea Tech are becoming important suppliers of towers, blades, generators, transformers, gearboxes, nacelle control systems, and cables.[38]

U.S. Market Attracts More Foreign Wind Turbine Manufacturers

The leading manufacturers of utility-scale wind turbines in the United States are shown in **Table 2**. In 2011, nearly two dozen wind turbine manufacturers—a five-fold increase in six years— installed nearly 3,500 new turbines nationwide, generating 6,800 MW of new capacity.[39] This was down from the 2009 peak, when some 5,700 new wind turbines were installed, adding nearly 10,000 MW of new utility-scale wind capacity.[40] Since the inception of utility-scale wind energy production, U.S. electric generators have installed more than 40,000 turbines with approximately 52,000 MW of capacity. In 2011, GE continued to lead in the number of new wind turbine installations, although its market share has declined over time.[41]

---

[37] Joanna Lewis, *Can Green Sunrise Industries Lead the Drive into Recovery? The Case of the Wind Power Industry in China and India*, United Nations Industrial Development Organization, 2010, p. 7, http://www.unido.org/fileadmin/ user_media/Publications/RSF_DPR/WP202009_Ebook.pdf.

[38] Joanna I. Lewis, *Building a National Wind Turbine Industry: Experiences from China, India, and South Korea*, Georgetown University, Int. J. Technology and Globalization, Vol 5, Nos. 3/4, 2011, pp. 290-293, http://www.china.tu-berlin.de/fileadmin/fg57/SS_2012/Umwelt/Lewis_windenery.pdf. For more information on the major players in the South Korean wind industry, see a report by the Maine International Trade Center, *"Opportunities for Maine Companies in Korean New and Renewable Energy (NRE) Markets,"* pp, 7-9, November 2010. http://www.mitc.com/ PDFs/RenewableEnergyinKorea_Report.pdf.

[39] AWEA, *U.S. Wind Industry Annual Market Report 2011*, p. 7.

[40] Ryan Wiser and Mark Bolinger, *2011 Wind Technologies Market Report*, Lawrence Berkeley National Laboratory, August 2012, p. 15, http://www1.eere.energy.gov/wind/pdfs/2011_wind_technologies_market_report.pdf.

[41] AWEA's 3rd Quarter 2012 Market Report found that total installations through the first nine months of 2012 reached 4,728 MW, compared to 3,370 for the same period in 2011.

Table 2. Annual Wind Turbine Installations in the United States

Top 10 Manufacturers by Selected Years, Ranked by Number Installed in 2011

Original Equipment Manufacturer (OEM)/Assembler[a]	Location of Headquarters	2005 (# of Turbines)	2009 (# of Turbines)	2010 (# of Turbines)	2011 (# of Turbines)
GE Energy	United States	954	2,663	1,679	1,252
Vestas	Denmark	403	830	75	952
Siemens	Germany	0	505	360	534
Suzlon[b]	India	8	344	201	159
Mitsubishi	Japan	190	491	146	133
Nordex	Germany	0	25	8	115
Clipper	United States	1	242	28	103
REpower	Germany	0	165	34	84
Gamesa	Spain	25	300	282	77
Alstom	France	0	0	0	25
All Others		33	200	129	30
Total		1,614	5,765	2,942	3,464

Source: AWEA, U.S. Wind Industry Annual Market Report, 2009, 2010, and 2011. The number of turbines is based on data compiled by AWEA and is accurate as of December 17, 2012, but is subject to revision.

a.   An OEM designs the turbine, typically assembles the nacelle, and sells the completed unit to developers.

b.   Suzlon acquired 100% of REpower during 2011. The two firms jointly had 243 installations in 2011.

Wind Turbine Components, Raw Materials, Global Supply Chain, and U.S. Manufacturing Capacity

Wind Turbine Components

A wind turbine is a collection of operating systems that convert energy from wind to produce electricity. Utility-scale wind turbines are massive, complex pieces of machinery which come in many sizes and configurations. Wind turbine blades range in size from 34 to 55 meters, the hub can weigh 8 to 10 tons, and towers are usually 80-100 meters tall and weigh 55 to 70 tons. According to AWEA, the installation of over 5,700 turbines in the United States in 2009 required industrial manufacturers to supply 17,000 blades and tower sections, approximately 3.2 million bolts, 36,000 miles of rebar, and 1.7 million cubic yards of concrete.[42]

---

[42] AWEA, *Anatomy of a Wind Turbine*, http://www.awea.org/issues/supply_chain/Anatomy-of-a-Wind-Turbine.cfm.

In simple terms, as shown in **Figure 1**, the major components in a wind turbine consist of:

- a rotor comprising four principal components—the blade, the blade extender, the hub, and the pitch drive system;

- a nacelle, the external shell or structure resting atop the tower containing and housing the controller, gearbox, generator, large bearings, connecting shafts, and electronic components that allow the turbine to monitor changes in wind speed and direction;

Figure 1. Wind Turbine Overview

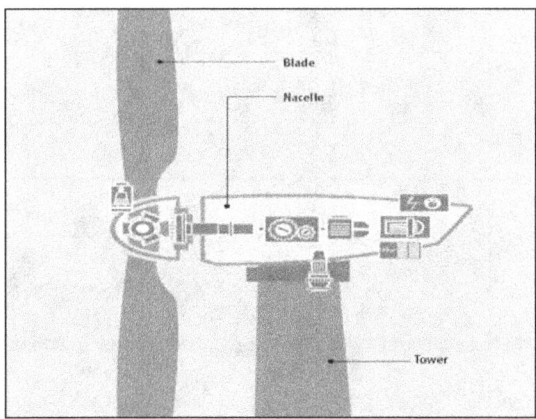

Source: Wind Directions, *"Supply Chain: The Race to Meet Demand,"* January/February 2007

- a tower, normally made of rolled steel tube sections that are bolted together to provide the support system for the blades and nacelle; and,

- other components, including transformers, circuit breakers, fiber optic cables, and ground-mounted electrical equipment.[43]

Beyond the major components, there are many subcomponents in a wind turbine. The percentages shown in **Figure 2** indicate the costs of the components relative to the overall cost of a turbine. The tower, for example, is over 26% of the total cost of a wind turbine, rotor blades 22%, the gearbox 13%, and the other components 5% or less.

---

[43] A detailed description of the components in a wind turbine can be found in *Wind Turbine Development: Location of Manufacturing Activity*, by George Sterzinger and Matt Svrcek, Renewable Energy Policy Project, September 2004. http://www.repp.org/articles/static/1/binaries/WindLocator.pdf.

Figure 2. Wind Turbine Components

Contribution of main parts as a percentage of overall costs based on a REpower MM92 Turbine

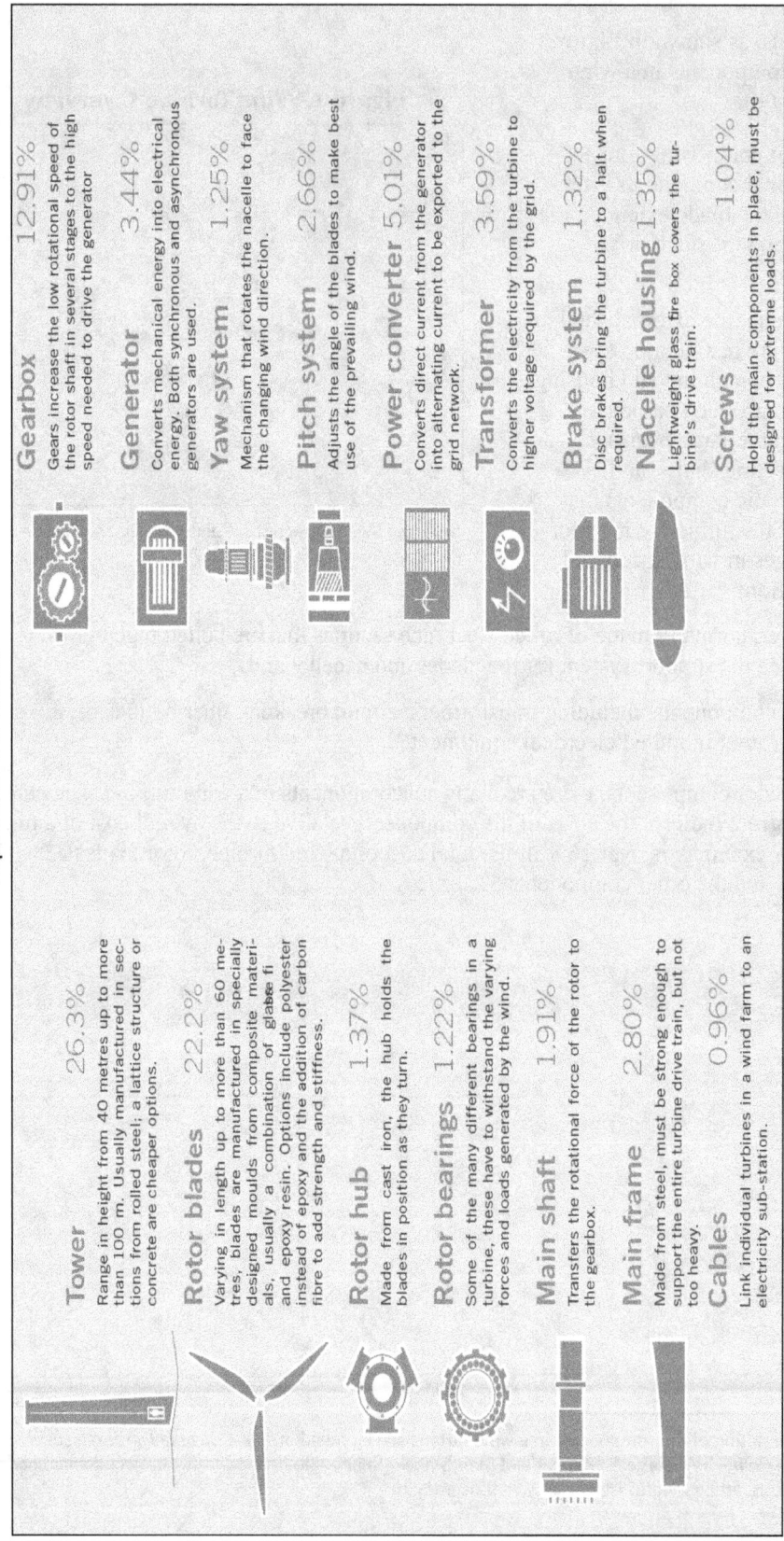

Tower 26.3%
Range in height from 40 metres up to more than 100 m. Usually manufactured in sections from rolled steel; a lattice structure or concrete are cheaper options.

Rotor blades 22.2%
Varying in length up to more than 60 metres, blades are manufactured in specially designed moulds from composite materials, usually a combination of glass fibre and epoxy resin. Options include polyester instead of epoxy and the addition of carbon fibre to add strength and stiffness.

Rotor hub 1.37%
Made from cast iron, the hub holds the blades in position as they turn.

Rotor bearings 1.22%
Some of the many different bearings in a turbine, these have to withstand the varying forces and loads generated by the wind.

Main shaft 1.91%
Transfers the rotational force of the rotor to the gearbox.

Main frame 2.80%
Made from steel, must be strong enough to support the entire turbine drive train, but not too heavy.

Cables 0.96%
Link individual turbines in a wind farm to an electricity sub-station.

Gearbox 12.91%
Gears increase the low rotational speed of the rotor shaft in several stages to the high speed needed to drive the generator

Generator 3.44%
Converts mechanical energy into electrical energy. Both synchronous and asynchronous generators are used.

Yaw system 1.25%
Mechanism that rotates the nacelle to face the changing wind direction.

Pitch system 2.66%
Adjusts the angle of the blades to make best use of the prevailing wind.

Power converter 5.01%
Converts direct current from the generator into alternating current to be exported to the grid network.

Transformer 3.59%
Converts the electricity from the turbine to higher voltage required by the grid.

Brake system 1.32%
Disc brakes bring the turbine to a halt when required.

Nacelle housing 1.35%
Lightweight glass fire box covers the turbine's drive train.

Screws 1.04%
Hold the main components in place, must be designed for extreme loads.

Source: Wind Directions, *"Supply Chain: The Race to Meet Demand,"* January/February 2007.

Wind turbines vary greatly in size and are getting larger as technology advances. They have grown from dozens of kilowatts in the early 1980s to as large as 7 MW.[44] Most land-based wind turbines are in the 1.5 MW to 3 MW range.[45] Components also change as technology improves. European and U.S. wind turbine manufacturers have invested heavily over the decades in developing their respective turbine technologies, leading to improvements in the efficiency of wind blades and turbines and longer turbine life. New wind turbine manufacturers, especially from China, are not yet globally competitive. According to recent research, they generally lack state-of-the-art technology, focus mainly on producing smaller turbines, and experience significant quality control problems.[46] Raw materials availability and changing commodity prices of raw materials used in wind turbines affect production costs.[47] A typical wind turbine is made primarily of steel (about 90% by weight) (see **Table 3**). Aluminum and other light-weight composites are also important, particularly for blade manufacturing. Other core materials include pre-stressed concrete, copper, and fiberglass. Turbines also utilize permanent magnets, cast iron, carbon fiber, rubber, epoxy, ferrite, brass, ceramics, and Teflon.[48]

Table 3. Raw Materials Requirements for Wind Turbines

based on a 1.5MW Wind Turbine by % of Weight, including blades and towers

	Steel	Fiberglass	Copper	Concrete	Adhesive	Aluminum	Core Materials
Weight %	89.1%	5.8%	1.6%	1.3%	1.1%	0.8%	0.4%

Source: U.S. Department of Energy, *20% Wind Energy by 2030*, p. 63, July 2008

Global Wind Turbine Assembly Supply Chain

Wind turbines are manufactured by original equipment manufacturers, or OEMs, which design, assemble, and brand their products. Similar to automobile assemblers that make a car or truck, OEMs are mostly system integrators. Assemblers must bring together an estimated 8,000 precision parts and components to produce a wind turbine.[49] One supplier might roll large plates of steel into the towers that support the turbine. A second company might make the turbine blades from special carbon fiber materials, and a third might manufacture the electronic computerized

---

[44] The German manufacturer Enercon has built the world's largest turbine model to date, the Enercon E-126, which can generate up to 7 MW of power.

[45] Economic and Workforce Development Program California Community Colleges, *Wind Turbine Technicians*, September 2009, p. 35, http://www.coeccc.net/Environmental_Scans/wind_scan_sw_09.pdf.

[46] Chi-Jen Yang, Eric Williams, and Jonas Monast, *Wind Power: Barriers and Policy Solutions*, Nicholas School of the Environment at Duke University, November 2008, pp. 14-15. http://nicholasinstitute.duke.edu/climate/electricity/wind-power-barriers-and-policy-solutions.

[47] Jacob Funk Kirkegaard, Thilo Hanemann, and Lutz Weischer, *It Should Be a Breeze: Harnessing the Potential of Open Trade and Investment Flows in the Wind Energy Industry*, Peterson Institute for International Economics, December 2010, p. 41, http://www.iie.com/publications/wp/wp09-14.pdf.

[48] David Wilburn, *Wind Energy in the United States and Materials Required for the Land-Based Wind Turbine Industry From 2010 through 2030*, U.S. Geological Survey, Scientific Investigations Report 2011-5036, 2011, pp. 7-8, http://pubs.usgs.gov/sir/2011/5036/sir2011-5036.pdf.

[49] Gloria Ayee, Marcy Lowe, and Gary Gereffi, et al., *Manufacturing Climate Solutions Carbon Reducing Technologies and U.S. Jobs*, Center on Globalization Governance and Competitiveness, Wind Power, September 22, 2009, p. 10, http://www.cggc.duke.edu/environment/climatesolutions/greeneconomy_Ch11_WindPower.pdf.

---

control systems. Each of these components might be produced domestically, might be assembled domestically from imported inputs, or might be imported as an assembled product.[50]

Tier 1 and Tier 2 Wind Turbine Component Suppliers

Many suppliers and specialty firms are part of this complex global supply chain. Tier 1 suppliers make large components such as towers, hubs, blades, or gearboxes. They include firms such as LM Wind (blades), SKF (bearings), and Winergy (gearboxes). Tier 2 suppliers produce subassemblies such as ladders, fiberglass, control systems, hydraulics, power electronics, fasteners, resin, machine parts, or motors. They include companies such as American Roller Bearings (power transmission bearings), Cardinal Fasteners (structural fasteners), and Timken (power transmission bearings).

Manufacturing Strategies

A wind turbine is a significant investment. Researchers at the Lawrence Berkeley National Laboratory reported that wind turbine transaction price quotes can range from as low as $900/kilowatt (kW) to a high of $1,400/kW,[51] meaning that an average 2 MW turbine would cost between $1.8 million and $2.8 million, plus installation costs.

Each wind turbine assembler uses different sourcing strategies and levels of vertical integration. Some produce almost all major components internally or through subsidiaries, while others outsource many of their critical components.[52] For instance, some manufacturers produce blades, generators, or gearboxes in-house, while others opt for outside suppliers. Hundreds of smaller companies make specialized parts such as clutches, rotor bearings, fasteners, sensors, and gears for the wind industry.[53] Illustrative examples of some of the thousands of components in a modern wind turbine are shown in **Table 4**.

Very high levels of expertise and specialization are required of wind turbine suppliers, with the level of precision similar to that of the aerospace industry. Turbine manufacturers often establish relationships with suppliers in the interest of quality, as a failure in a turbine part can be very expensive to fix. Wind turbines are expected to survive largely unattended in extreme climactic

---

[50] BlueGreen Alliance, *Clean Energy Economy Report 2009*, June 15, 2009, p. 3, http://www.repp.org/articles/BGA_Repp.pdf.

[51] U.S. Department of Energy, *2011 Wind Technologies Market Report*, August 2012, p. 33.

[52] One analysis of vertical integration among wind OEMs indicates that Suzlon and Enercon have significant in-house production and high or very high levels of vertical integration; Siemens and Vestas fall in the middle; and GE is less vertically integrated than many other manufacturers, relying on outside suppliers for blades, gearboxes, generators, castings and forgings, and towers. Josh Lutton, *Wind Turbine Manufacturer Recommendations (Round 2)*, Woodlawn Associates, April 27, 2010, p. 6, http://www.woodlawnassociates.com/uploads/Woodlawn_Associates_WT_Recs_-_R2_100427.pdf.

[53] Dan Ancona and Jim McVeigh, *Wind Turbine—Materials and Manufacturing Fact Sheet*, Office of Industrial Technologies, U.S. Department of Energy. August 29, 2001. http://www.perihq.com/documents/WindTurbine-MaterialsandManufacturing_FactSheet.pdf.

---

conditions for a design life of as much as 20 years.[54] Product quality is also of concern to wind farm operators, as a malfunctioning turbine can reduce operating revenue.[55]

Table 4. Selected Wind Turbine Components

Towers:	Nacelle:	Foundation:
• Towers	• Nacelle Cover	• Rebar
• Ladders	• Nacelle Base	• Concrete
• Lifts	• Heat exchanger	• Casings
Rotor:	• Controllers	**Other:**
• Hub	• Generator	• Transformers
• Nose Cone	• Power Electronics	• Bolts/Fasteners
• Blades	• Lubricants	• Wire
• Pitch Mechanisms	• Filtration	• Paints and Coatings
• Drives	• Insulation	• Lighting Protection
• Bakes	• Gearbox	• Steelworking/Machining
• Rotary Union	• Pump	• Communication Devices
	• Drivetrain	• Control and Condition Monitoring Equipment
	• Ceramics	• Electrical Interface and Connections
	• Shaft	• Batteries
		• Bearings
		• Brakes

Source: AWEA, *Manufacturing Supplier Handbook for the Wind Energy Industry*, 2011, p. 29. http://www.awea.org/issues/supply_chain/upload/Supplier-Handbook.pdf

---

[54] Michelle Avis and Preben Maegaard, *Worldwide Wind Turbine Market and Manufacturing Trends*, Xmire, January 2008, p. 21, http://www.folkecenter.net/mediafiles/folkecenter/pdf/Market_and_Manufacturer_Trends.pdf.

[55] Manufacturers like Suzlon have experienced recent failures of their turbines. Reliability and performance are critical factors affecting shareholder value, the reputation, and future growth of any wind OEM.

U.S. Wind Turbine Manufacturing Facilities

At the end of 2011, the American Wind Energy Association reported that more than 470 wind turbine manufacturing facilities were located in the United States, up substantially from the 30-40 wind-related manufacturing facilities nationwide in 2004. Over that period, the number of tower plants increased from 6 to 18; blade facilities rose from 4 to 12; and, nacelle assembly facilities grew from 3 to 14.[56] Total investment in facilities to manufacture for the wind industry in the United States has exceeded $1.5 billion.[57]

Greater demand for wind turbines, cost savings related to transportation, and concern about the risks associated with currency fluctuations are among the reasons wind turbine and component manufacturers have opened new production facilities in the United States since 2005.[58] Even with increased domestic production capacity, wind turbine assemblers source parts and components on a worldwide basis, reflecting the industry's global supply chain. Many wind manufacturers with production facilities in the United States also produce elsewhere, typically in Europe and Asia.

U.S. Wind-Related Manufacturing Facilities, Number of Facilities by Selected Categories, December 2011
Towers 18
Blades 12
Nacelle Assembly 14
Fasteners 21
Bearings 21
Castings 14
Gearboxes 7
Generators 1
Source: AWEA.

Towers and Blades

Towers and blades were among the first wind products manufactured in the United States because they are large, expensive, and difficult to transport.[59] Thus, manufacturers find it easier and less costly to fabricate near their installation point. Many tower manufacturers in the United States are American companies and include firms such as Ameron, Trinity Structural Towers, DMI Industries, and Broadwind Towers. Foreign manufacturers, such as Gamesa and Vestas, also have located tower manufacturing facilities in the United States. In 2012, several major tower producers, including Otter Tail Corporation, Katana Summit, and DMI Industries, exited the sector or announced plans to scale back production. Suppliers of blades have increased their U.S. manufacturing capacity, with three times as many facilities in 2011 as in 2005. For example, LM Wind Power, headquartered in Denmark, is the largest supplier of blades in the world; it now

---

[56] AWEA provided these statistics to CRS via email on December 5, 2012.

[57] AWEA, *Policy and Manufacturing: Demand-Side Policies Will Fuel Growth in the Wind Manufacturing Sector*, 2011, p. 3, http://www.thenewnorth.com/resources/mwgpolicypaper.pdf.

[58] Andrew David, *Impact of Wind Energy Installations on Domestic Manufacturing and Trade*, U.S. International Trade Commission, July 2010, p. 7, http://www.usitc.gov/publications/332/working_papers/ID-25.pdf.

[59] Transporting wind turbines, which requires special trucks, railroad carriages, and cranes, is difficult because of their unusual weight, length, and shape. For example, a typical nacelle weighs between 50 and 70 tons. Blades can run from 110 feet to 145 feet. Towers can weigh 70 tons. According to some estimates, transportation costs can account for up to 20% of the installed cost of a wind turbine. Estimates from AWEA suggest that per-turbine transportation and logistics costs range from $100,000 to $150,000. For more information see, *The Logistics of Transporting Wind Turbines: Reducing Inefficiencies, Costs, and Community Impact by Streamlining the Supply Chain*, CN White Paper 2009, http://www.cn.ca/documents/WhitePapers/Transporting-Wind-Turbines-White-Paper-en.pdf.

---

produces blades at two U.S. manufacturing facilities.[60] Other blade manufacturers with U.S. production facilities include two American companies, TPI Composites and Molded Fiberglass. Both make blades for GE.

Turbine Nacelle Assembly

European OEMs, including Gamesa, Nordex, Siemens, and Vestas, have opened nacelle assembly plants in the United States in recent years.[61] Some started investing in the United States heavily after the American Recovery and Reinvestment Act (P.L. 111-5) passed in 2009.[62] Siemens and Nordex also opened their first U.S. nacelle assembly facilities in 2009. GE has three nacelle assembly facilities in the United States, all established prior to 2005, and also operates turbine component plants in China, Vietnam, and Europe. With the exception of DeWind, which was a German-owned manufacturer acquired by South Korea's Daewoo Shipbuilding & Marine Engineering Company in 2009, Asian manufacturers lag in establishing a U.S. nacelle manufacturing presence. Japanese-headquartered Mitsubishi had expected to open its first U.S. nacelle assembly plant in 2012, but has delayed the opening of that facility.[63] Other manufacturers, such as Suzlon, which idled its turbine rotor blade plant in Minnesota, have reduced their U.S. manufacturing presence.[64] **Appendix B** provides an overview of the varied investment strategies pursued by foreign-based wind turbine assemblers in the United States.

Other Wind Turbine Components

A more robust domestic manufacturing base for wind turbine components such as bearings, gearboxes, and power transmissions is also being established in the United States, albeit more slowly than for towers, blades, and nacelle assembly. Gearboxes and bearings are among the most critical components for any wind turbine manufacturer because failures in either of these parts mean the wind turbine will fail. Bearings for wind turbines are made by a few manufacturers, such as German-headquartered FAG[65] and U.S.-headquartered Timken.[66] Both have production capacity in the United States and operate factories in Europe and Asia. Gearboxes are also made by a relatively small number of companies, such as Winergy (now part of Siemens), which established U.S. production capacity in Illinois in 2009.[67] Winergy also makes gearboxes in

---

[60] LM Wind Power, LM Wind Power Group—Facts, http://www.lmwindpower.com/upload/lmwp_factsheet_groupuk_020511.pdf.

[61] AWEA, *U.S. Wind Industry Annual Market Report, 2011,* 2012, p. 38.

[62] The American Recovery and Reinvestment Act (ARRA) of 2009 included grants, loans, and tax credits.

[63] Chisaki Watanabe, "Mitsubishi Heavy to Suspend U.S. Wind Factory on Sluggish Demand," April 2, 2012.

[64] Suzlon, which once employed more than 500 U.S. workers who made rotor blades used in wind turbines in Pipestone, MN, now has about 30 employees there, engaged primarily in blade repair work and customer service. Debra Fitzgerald, "Suzlon Shifts Focus of Pipestone Plant," *Pipestone County StarOnline*, February 15, 2012.

[65] FAG, a unit of the Schaeffler Group, has produced bearings for wind turbines for over 30 years. It has a U.S. factory in Joplin, MO. See FAG, *"Expertise in Bearing Technology and Service for Wind Turbines,"* March 2010, http://www.schaeffler.com/remotemedien/media/_shared_media/library/schaeffler_2/brochure/downloads_1/pwe_de_en.pdf.

[66] Timken, headquartered in Ohio, is a global supplier of bearings with a full line for the wind industry. Timken produces ultra-large bore bearings for wind turbines in South Carolina and also operates wind-bearing production manufacturing facilities in Brazil, China, and Romania. It also provides clean steel for wind energy from its facilities in Canton, OH. See http://www.timken.com/en-us/about/Pages/Locations.aspx.

[67] "Siemens & Winergy Open Wind Turbine Manufacturing Plant," *Renewable Energy World.com*, August 31, 2009. http://www.renewableenergyworld.com/rea/news/article/2009/08/siemens-winergy-open-turbine-manufacturing-plant.

Europe, China, and India.[68] Manufacturers of power transmissions, power converters, composite coatings, and sensors have also located wind-related production facilities in the United States.

Outlook

There is now increasing evidence that falling natural gas prices, and uncertainty over the future of the PTC, has diminished manufacturers' interest in establishing more wind-related production facilities in the United States. An analysis by the National Renewable Energy Laboratory (NREL) reported that in 2011, 16 new turbine and component manufacturing facilities opened across the nation, compared to 13 in 2010.[69] In 2012, some manufacturers delayed implementing announced plans for new factories or expansion of existing ones, and several companies reduced their U.S. workforce.

An Emerging U.S. Wind Manufacturing Corridor

A concentration of tower, blade, and nacelle assembly plants is found in the central part of the United States, as shown in **Figure 3**. Texas, Iowa, Colorado, Arkansas, and Kansas are positioned near sites that are favorable for wind power generation, enabling manufacturers there to minimize transportation challenges and costs. In addition, wind turbine assemblers and tower and blade manufacturers have been attracted to these states by incentive packages including property tax abatements, sales tax reductions, low-interest loans, and support for worker training. Other wind-related manufacturing facilities are located in Pennsylvania, Michigan, and Ohio, where the decline of automotive and heavy industrial manufacturing has left behind a workforce with prior experience with steel, assembly lines, robotics, and other aspects of heavy manufacturing.[70]

---

[68] Winergy, Production Locations, http://www.winergy-group.com/cms/website.php?id=/en/about-winergy/locations.htm.

[69] Ryan Wiser and Mark Bolinger, *2011 Wind Technologies Market Report*, National Renewable Energy Laboratory, August 2012, p. 16, http://www1.eere.energy.gov/wind/pdfs/2011_wind_technologies_market_report.pdf.

[70] AWEA reports at least 30 facilities in Michigan, more than 50 companies in Ohio, and about 15 factories in Pennsylvania now manufacture components for the wind industry. AWEA, *State-specific wind energy fact sheets, updated through the 3rd Quarter 2012*, http://www.awea.org/learnabout/publications/factsheets/factsheets_state.cfm.

Figure 3. Wind Turbine Manufacturing Facilities in the United States

By Tower, Blade, and Turbine Nacelle Assembly, 2011

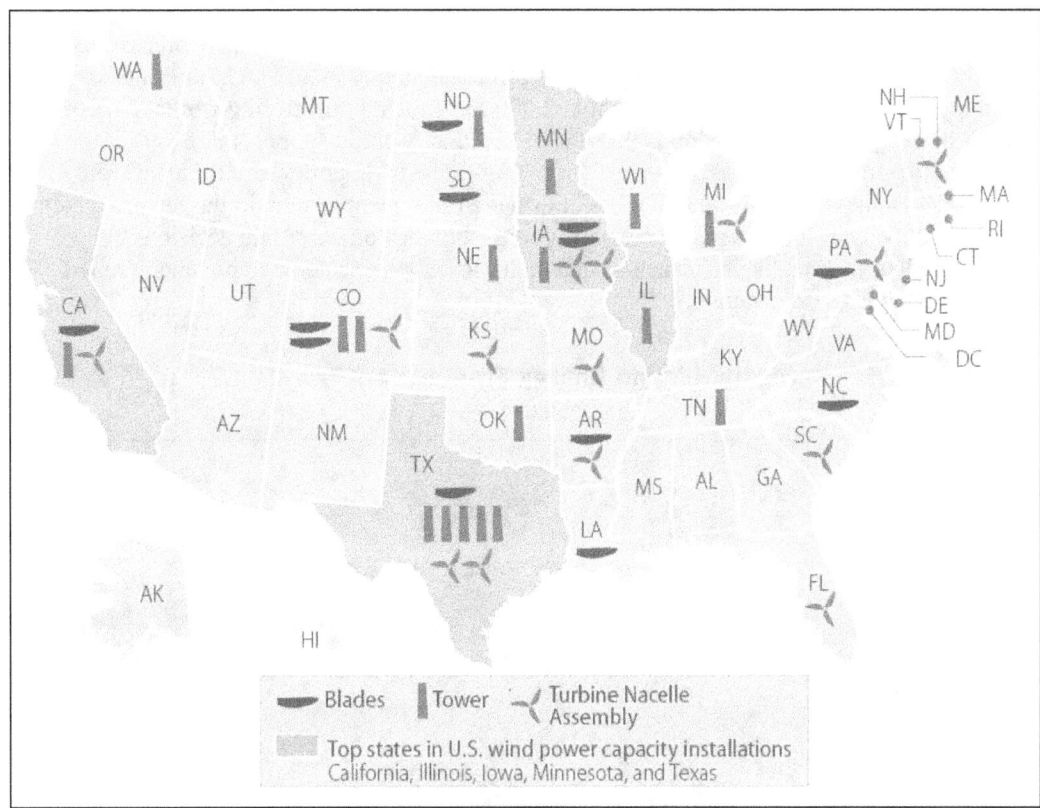

Source: CRS based on data from AWEA. The map shows 44 online tower, blade, and turbine nacelle assembly facilities at year-end 2011. It does not show the more than 400 facilities that produce wind components such as power transmissions, generators, gearboxes, or bearings.

U.S. Wind Turbine Manufacturing Employment

In 2011, the wind turbine manufacturing sector supported an estimated 30,000 manufacturing jobs nationwide. This was only about one-fourth of U.S. employment related to wind energy manufacturing. The majority (some 60%) of the 75,000 full-time workers employed directly and indirectly in the wind power industry at the end of 2011 worked in finance and consulting services, contracting and engineering services, project development, and transportation and logistics.[71] About 4,200 jobs were in construction and 4,000 were in operations and maintenance. The number of manufacturing jobs has been relatively flat over the past three years, even as total employment in wind energy declined, according to figures from AWEA (see **Figure 4**).[72]

---

[71] AWEA employment data were provided to CRS via email on December 4, 2012, and are based on surveys and modeling.

[72] AWEA, *U.S. Wind Industry Annual Market Report, 2011*, 2011, p. 45. AWEA is the only source of nationwide employment statistics, as the U.S. government does not currently track employment in the wind industry. Measurement of employment in wind turbine manufacturing is complicated by the fact that no single industry codes exist to isolate wind power establishments or wind turbine and wind components establishments. The North American Industry Classification System (NAICS) places wind turbine manufacturers within the Turbine and Turbine Generator Set Units (continued...)

Wind turbine manufacturing is responsible for a very small share of the 11.7 million domestic manufacturing jobs in 2011, well under 1%. It seems unlikely, even if there were a substantial increase in U.S. manufacturing capacity, that wind turbine manufacturing will become a major source of manufacturing employment. In 2008, the U.S. Department of Energy forecast that if wind power were to provide 20% of the nation's electrical supply in 2030, U.S. turbine assembly and component plants could support roughly 32,000 full-time manufacturing workers in 2026.[73] AWEA's more optimistic projection is that the wind industry could support three to four times as many manufacturing workers as it does now if a long-term stable policy environment were in place, which implies a total of 80,000 jobs.[74] Further employment growth in the sector is likely to depend not only upon future demand for wind energy, but also on corporate decisions about where to produce towers, blades, nacelles, and their most sophisticated components, such as gearboxes, bearings, and generators.

Figure 4. Wind Energy Employment Trends

2007-2011

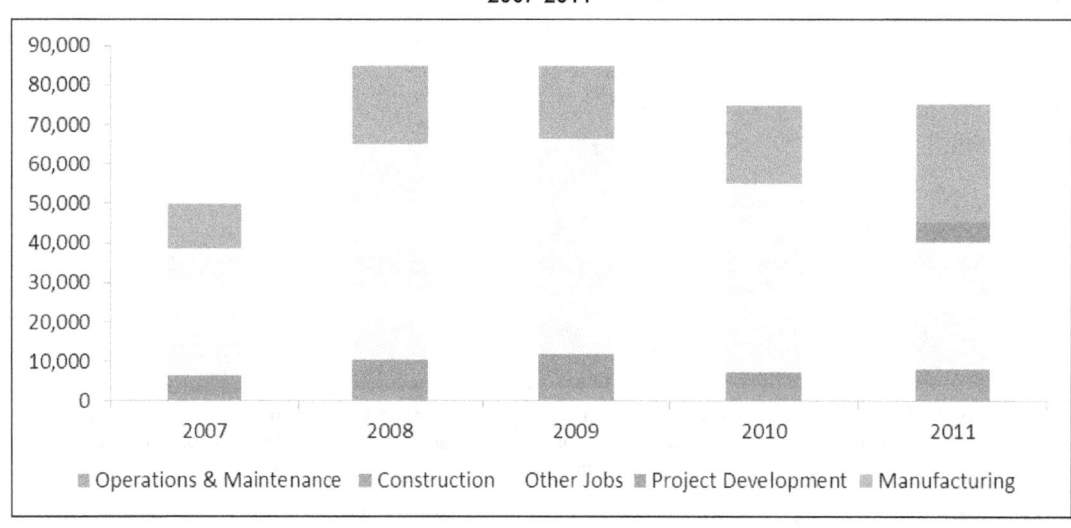

Source: AWEA, *U.S. Wind Industry Annual Market Report*, 2011.

Note: Other jobs include financial and consultant services, developers and development services, contracting and engineering services, and transportation and logistics. Project development employment is only available beginning in 2011.

(...continued)

manufacturing industry (NAICS 333611), which comprises "establishments primarily engaged in manufacturing turbines (except aircraft) and complete turbine generator set units, such as steam, hydraulic, gas, and wind." BLS reports 29,070 total jobs in this industry in 2011, with employment increasing every year since 2005, when it had 19,500 employees.

[73] U.S. Department of Energy, *20% Wind Energy by 2030: Increasing Wind Energy's Contribution to U.S. Electricity Supply*, July 2008, p. 207, http://www.20percentwind.org/20percent_wind_energy_report_revOct08.pdf. DOE estimates are based on major component assumptions that by 2030 80% of blades, 50% of towers, and 42% of turbines installed in the United States would be manufactured domestically.

[74] AWEA, *Policy and Manufacturing: Demand-Side Policies Will Fuel Growth in the Wind Manufacturing Sector*, 2011, p. 9, http://www.thenewnorth.com/resources/mwgpolicypaper.pdf.

Wind Turbine Equipment Trade

U.S. Imports

As part of their global business strategies, wind turbine manufacturers continue to source a significant share of components outside the United States.[75] Imports of wind-powered generating sets, the main wind category covering fully assembled wind turbines and including other components such as blades and hubs when they are imported with the nacelle, grew from $482.5 million in 2005 to a peak of $2.5 billion in 2008. In 2009, imports of wind-powered generating sets dropped to $2.3 billion, then fell by another 46% to $1.2 billion, before rising by 1% in 2011 (see **Figure 5**).[76] An analysis of U.S. wind equipment trade by the U.S. International Trade Commission identified several explanations for the recent decline in U.S. imports of wind-powered generating sets, which include fewer wind turbine installations; decreasing prices; and the opening of new production facilities in the United States.[77]

The overwhelming majority (95%) of imported wind-powered generating sets come from Europe. In 2011, Denmark was the leading source of wind-powered generating sets, making up more than half (55%) of all imports into the United States. Italy, Germany, and Spain combined accounted for another 40% (see **Figure 5**). China and India accounted for 2% and 1% of imports, respectively, in 2011.

It appears that South Korean wind turbine manufacturers like Samsung, Hyosung, and Unison have ambitions to become leading exporters to the U.S. market and other global markets.[78] Even though China is home to 60 wind energy manufacturers, including several ranked among the largest in the world, it has exported only a small number of wind turbines, $351 million by value worldwide in 2011. However, Chinese manufacturers such as Goldwind, Sinovel, United Power, and Mingyang are actively seeking to expand their foreign sales. Between 2008 and 2011, 11 Chinese OEMs exported 194 wind turbines, based on one estimate, with the United States accounting for 59% of the installations.[79] Also, European turbine assemblers such as Vestas are

---

[75] Gerald Susman and Amy Glasmeier, "*Industry Structure and Company Strategies of Major Domestic and Foreign Wind and Solar Energy Manufacturers: Opportunities for Supply Chain Development in Appalachia*," Smeal College of Business, November 20, 2009, p. 38, http://www.arc.gov/assets/research_reports/WindandSolarEnergy.pdf.

[76] Precisely tracking trade flows in the wind industry is complicated because the standard Harmonized Commodity Coding and Classification System (HS) does not have separate harmonized trade categories for all wind turbines and their components. Wind turbines and components are classified under several HS codes. Wind-powered generating sets (HS 8502.31) is the main category, which includes fully assembled wind turbines, but may also cover components such as blades and hubs when they are imported with the nacelle. However, when imported separately other individual turbine components (e.g., generators (HS 8501.64), towers (7308.20), and blades and other components (8412.90 and 8503.00) may be traded under other HS headings. Importantly, goods that are not used in wind turbines are also included in these categories. But, the ITC reports, wind accounts for a significant portion of trade in each dual use category and appears to be a major driver of import growth in those HS headings. For a complete discussion see, USITC, "*Wind Turbines: Industry and Trade Summary*," by Andrew David, June 2009.

[77] Andrew David, *Shifts in U.S. Wind Turbine Equipment Trade in 2010*, U.S. International Trade Commission, USITC Executive Briefing on Trade, June 2011, http://www.usitc.gov/publications/332/executive_briefings/wind_EBOT_commission_review_final2.pdf.

[78] Dr. Rimtalg Lee, *Status and Forecast of Wind Energy In Korea*, San Francisco, CA, March 2, 2009, pp. 7-9, http://www.asiapacificpartnership.org/pdf/PGTTF/wind-event/March_2/StatusnForecastofWindEnrgyKorea.pdf.

[79] Ginger Gardiner, "Windpower 2012 Report," *Composites Technology*, August 1, 2012, http://www.compositesworld.com/articles/windpower-2012-report. BTM Consult reports total capacity of Chinese (continued...)

---

now looking to open plants in China to supply the Chinese market, and possibly global markets.[80] Concerns about the quality of Chinese-made turbines and parts have prevented more rapid adoption of Chinese components. This may change as Chinese wind turbine products improve and as more foreign manufacturers establish operations in China.

Figure 5. U.S. Imports of Wind-Powered Generating Sets, Select Countries
2005-2011

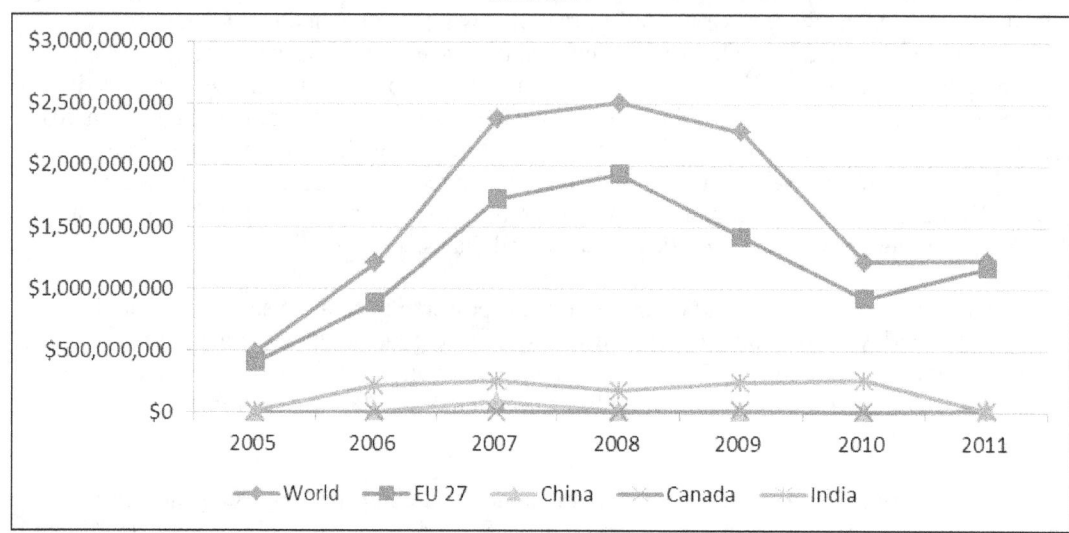

Source: Global Trade Atlas. These statistics only cover wind-powered generating sets (HS 8502.31), not components such as blades, towers or gearboxes imported separately.

Note: The import statistics are shown on a domestic consumption basis.

China's efforts to foster wind turbine manufacturing have been an irritant in the bilateral relationship. The United Steelworkers (USW) filed a claim in September 2010 that China's green technology policies are direct violations of China's World Trade Organization (WTO) obligations.[81] In June 2011, after the World Trade Organization panel upheld a U.S. complaint, the Office of the U.S. Trade Representative (USTR) announced that China will end a program of wind power equipment grants that required Chinese wind turbine manufacturers that received them to use domestic parts and components instead of foreign-made parts and components.[82]

(...continued)

wind turbine exports increased to 222 MW in 2011 from almost 17 MW in 2008.

[80] Vestas, Company Structure, Vestas China, http://www.vestas.com/en/about-vestas/company-structure/vestas-china.aspx.

[81] United Steelworkers, *United Steelworkers' Section 301 Petition Demonstrates China's Green Technology Practices Violate WTO Rules*, http://assets.usw.org/releases/misc/section-301.pdf.

[82] China's Special Fund for Wind Power Equipment Manufacturing provided individual grants ranging from $6.7 million to $22.5 million to Chinese wind turbine manufacturers in exchange for using domestic parts and components instead of imported ones. For more information on China's Special Fund see USTR's June 7, 2011 press release, "China Ends Wind Power Equipment Subsidies Challenged by the United States in WTO Dispute," http://insidetrade.com/iwpfile.html?file=jun2011%2Fwto2011_1868a.pdf.

Besides the USW complaint, the U.S. wind tower industry has been involved in an ongoing trade case. In December 2011, the Wind Tower Trade Coalition, representing four U.S. manufacturers of steel towers for wind turbines,[83] filed anti-dumping and countervailing duty (CVD) petitions with the U.S. Department of Commerce (DOC) and the International Trade Commission (ITC), alleging that Chinese and Vietnamese makers of wind towers have injured U.S. producers by selling their products in the United States at below-market prices. In May 2012, DOC ruled that Chinese exporters of utility scale wind towers are being unfairly subsided and announced preliminary CVD rates ranging from 13.74% to 26%.[84] In July 2012, DOC issued an affirmative preliminary anti-dumping ruling that could impose additional duties as high as 73% on Chinese towers imported into the United States.[85] Final determinations are scheduled for early 2013. If the dumping and subsidy cases lead to significant tariffs, the rulings may impact the magnitude and source countries of tower imports from China to the United States in future years.

U.S. imports of other wind-related equipment, such as towers and blades, followed a similar pattern to wind-powered generating sets, with increases from 2005 to 2008 followed by a drop in 2009, then again in 2010, with a rise in 2011. But although more of these large components are being produced domestically, imports remain significant. China, Mexico, Vietnam, and South Korea were the main sources of imported towers and lattice masts in 2011.[86] China, Mexico, and Canada led in blade imports in 2011.[87] Some turbine components, such as bearings and gearboxes, are relatively easier to transport, and wind turbine assemblers might be more likely to continue to use global sourcing strategies for these less bulky components.

Domestic Content

Estimates indicate that U.S. content in recent years has increased to nearly 70% of the value of the average wind turbine installed in the United States.[88] In an August 2012 report, analysts at the Lawrence Berkeley National Laboratory calculated that the share of parts manufactured domestically nearly doubled from around 35% in 2005-2006 to 67% in 2011.[89]

---

[83] The Wind Tower Trade Coalition comprises Broadwind Towers of Manitowoc, WI; DMI Industries of Fargo, ND; Katana Summit LLC of Columbus, NE; and, Trinity Structural Towers of Dallas, TX.

[84] In the countervailing duty case, DOC found that Chinese wind tower manufacturers, including CS Wind and Titan Wind, benefited from Chinese subsidy programs. See *Commerce Preliminarily Finds Countervailable Subsidization of Imports of Utility Scale Wind Towers from the People's Republic of China (China)*, May 30, 2012, http://ia.ita.doc.gov/ download/factsheets/factsheet-prc-towers-cvd-prelim-20120530.pdf.

[85] The DOC preliminarily assessed duties include 30.93% on Chengxi Shipyard, 20.85% on Titan Wind Energy, 26.25% on CS Wind Corporation, Guodian United Power Technology Baoding, and Sinovel, and a China-wide rate of 72.69%. For a DOC anti-dumping fact sheet, see U.S. Department of Commerce, International Trade Administration, *Commerce Preliminarily Finds Dumping of Imports of Utility Scale Wind Towers*, July 27, 2012, http://ia.ita.doc.gov/ download/factsheets/factsheet-china-vietnam-uswt-ad-prelim-20120727.pdf.

[86] The Harmonized Tariff Schedule classifies wind towers under towers and lattice masts (HS 7308.20). Not all the towers in this category are wind towers.

[87] Wind blades are classified under the tariff lines for parts of other engines and motor (HS 8412.90) and parts of generators (HS 8503.00). Not all shipments in this category are wind-related.

[88] Precisely how many wind turbine components are made in the United States and how many are imported is a debatable issue. U.S. content need only be disclosed on a few products, namely automobiles, textiles, wool, and fur products. For most other products, no law requires disclosure of domestic content. In the case of automobiles, the American Automobile Labeling Act (AALA) requires automobile assemblers to include labels that specify the percentage value of the U.S./Canadian parts content of each vehicle sold in the United States.

[89] Ryan Wiser and Mark Bolinger, *2011 Wind Technologies Market Report*, Lawrence Berkeley National Laboratory, (continued...)

Public statements by major wind turbine assemblers appear to support the view that U.S.-made turbines now contain a larger share of domestic content than in previous years. For example, Gamesa reports that its domestic content on U.S.-made wind turbines is upwards of 65% and it has a local supply goal of 75%.[90] Vestas has stated domestic content in one class of its wind turbines has grown to 80%, and it expects to increase the overall percentage to 90%, including components and suppliers.[91] The *2011 Wind Technologies Market Report* notes "a growing amount of the equipment used in wind power projects has been sourced domestically in recent years. Whether that trend continues in the future may depend on the size and stability of the U.S. wind power market as well as the manufacturing strategies of emerging wind turbine manufacturers from Asia and elsewhere. "[92]

U.S. Exports

Future growth of the U.S. wind turbine industry also depends on foreign markets. A goal of the Obama Administration is to demonstrably increase renewable energy and energy efficiency exports like wind turbines.[93] Exports of wind-powered generating sets from the United States to the world remain relatively small, especially in comparison to imports, at only $255 million in 2011, up from $3.6 million in 2005 (see **Figure 6**).[94]

(...continued)

August 2012, p. 23, http://www1.eere.energy.gov/wind/pdfs/2011_wind_technologies_market_report.pdf.

[90] Michael A. Peck, *Briefing by Michael A. Peck to the Maryland Commission on Oversight of Public-Private Partnerships*, MAPA Group, September 28, 2011, p. 9, http://www.docstoc.com/docs/99871353/Briefing-by-Michael-A-Peck-to-the-Maryland-Commission-on-.

[91] U.S. Congress, House Committee on Ways and Means, Subcommittee on Select Revenue Measures, *Written Comments for the Record: Hearing for Certain Expiring Tax Credits*, 112th Cong., 2nd sess., April 26, 2012, p. 3, http://waysandmeans.house.gov/uploadedfiles/vestas_american_wind_tech._inc._fc42612.pdf.

[92] Ryan Wiser and Mark Bolinger, *2011 Wind Technologies Market Report*, Lawrence Berkeley National Laboratory, August 2012, p. 24, http://www1.eere.energy.gov/wind/pdfs/2011_wind_technologies_market_report.pdf.

[93] National Export Initiative, *Renewable Energy and Energy Efficiency Export Initiative*, December 2010, http://export.gov/reee/eg_main_023036.asp.

[94] GTIS, Global Trade Atlas database (accessed December 11, 2012).

Figure 6. U.S. Exports of Wind-Powered Generating Sets

in millions of U.S. dollars, 2005-2011

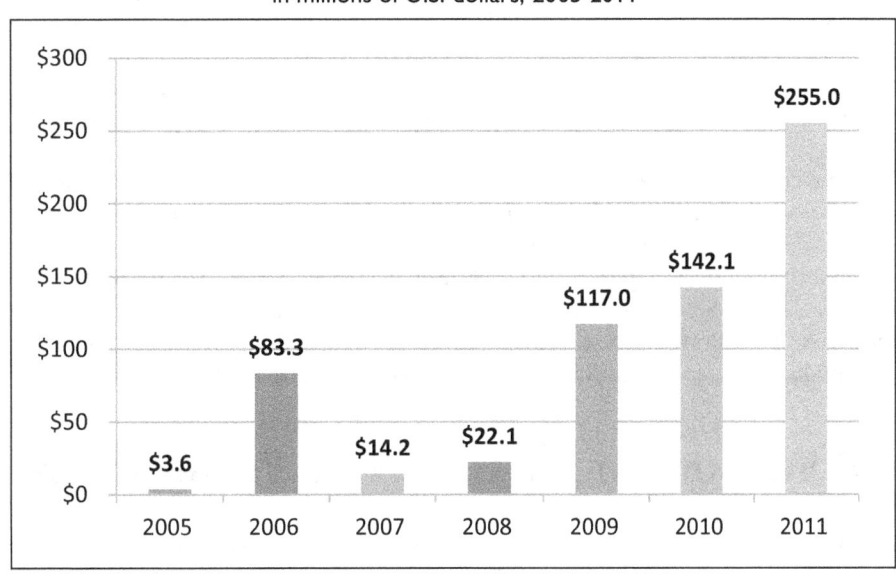

Source: Global Trade Atlas (accessed December 12, 2012).

Notes: These statistics only cover wind-powered generating sets, which refer to the complete nacelle and any items imported with the nacelle (HS 8502.31).

U.S. producers may turn to foreign markets to offset falling domestic demand because of increasing market uncertainty and overcapacity in U.S. wind turbine equipment manufacturing.[95] The Western Hemisphere may be especially attractive to U.S.-based exporters of wind turbine equipment. For instance, the expansion of the Canadian and Mexican wind turbine markets could increase export opportunities for companies with manufacturing operations in the United States, including GE, Siemens, Gamesa, and Vestas. [96] Brazil is the largest market in Latin America for wind power, which could provide U.S.-producers of nacelles and wind subcomponents with fresh export opportunities. A counter-trend is that wind turbine assemblers also are localizing production in the large Brazilian market, including manufacturers like GE and Gamesa.[97] Although considerably smaller, there are other growing markets in Central and South America that could buy more U.S. wind products, including Honduras, Uruguay, and Chile.

---

[95] Ryan Wiser and Mark Bolinger, *2011 Wind Technologies Market Report*, Lawrence Berkeley National Laboratory, August 2012, p. 17, http://www1.eere.energy.gov/wind/pdfs/2011_wind_technologies_market_report.pdf.

[96] Andrew S. David and Dennis Fravel, *U.S. Wind Turbine Export Opportunities in Canada and Latin America*, United States International Trade Commission, No ID—032, July 2012, p. 11-26, http://www.usitc.gov/publications/332/working_papers/ID-032_final.pdf.

[97] Ibid, pp. 23-32.

If U.S. manufacturers begin to export more wind turbine equipment, they will have to contend with import tariffs, non-tariff barriers, and domestic industry subsidies. Tariff rates in some major markets are disproportionately higher than U.S. tariffs. For instance, the U.S. duty rate for wind-powered generating sets is 2.5%, compared to 14% in Brazil, 8% in China, 7.5% in India, and 2.7% in the European Union.[98] Subsidies and non-tariff barriers in major overseas markets like China are another potential constraint on U.S. exports.[99]

Several U.S. government programs are designed to encourage the export of renewable energy products, such as direct loans provided to wind manufacturers by the Export-Import Bank of the United States.[100] Owing to the Ex-Im Banks's environmental export financing program, for example, Clipper Windpower exported 27 wind turbines to Mexico in 2010 based on a direct loan from the Ex-Im Bank of $80.7 million.[101] In 2011 and 2012, Ex-Im also extended loans of $22 million for 55 Northern Power wind turbines to Italy,[102] $159 million for 51 Gamesa wind turbines to Honduras,[103] and $32 million for 55 LM Wind Power wind blades to Brazil.[104]

Federal Support for the U.S. Wind Power Industry

Worldwide the wind power industry is driven by various types of government support, which range from tax credits to incentive policies like feed-in tariffs.[105] These incentives have been much larger in several foreign countries than in the United States, which has helped to spur the manufacturing of wind turbines in Europe and Asia. More recently, however, many countries—especially in Europe—have begun to reduce subsidies for renewables, including wind.[106]

---

[98] World Trade Organization, Tariff Analysis Online, http://www.wto.org/english/tratop_e/tariffs_e/tariff_data_e.htm.

[99] Clean energy policies in China, Japan, and South Korea are detailed in a November 2009 study by the Breakthrough Institute and the Information Technology & Innovation Foundation, *"Rising Tigers Sleeping Giant: Asian Nations Set to Dominate the Clean Energy Race by Out-Investing the United States"* http://thebreakthrough.org/blog/Rising_Tigers.pdf.

[100] More information about the Export-Import Bank's Environmental Exports Program can be accessed at http://www.exim.gov/products/policies/environment/success.cfm.

[101] Export-Import Bank of the United States, "Clipper Windpower Transaction is Named Ex-Im Bank Deal of the Year," press release, March 11, 2010, http://www.exim.gov/pressrelease.cfm/4EB6A01A-B9E1-FABF-D9409670AEB9668D/.

[102] Export-Import Bank of the United States, "Vermont Manufacturer Makes Largest U.S. Export Of Distributed Wind Turbines, Ex-Im Bank Guarantees Financing ," press release, May 26, 2011, http://www.exim.gov/newsandevents/releases/2011/vermont-manufacturer-makes-largest-u-s-export-of-distributed-wind-turbines-ex-im-bank-guarantees-financing.cfm.

[103] Craig O'Connor, *Financing Cleantech Exports: The Role of Ex-Im Bank*, Export-Import Bank of the United States, December 14, 2011, p. 15. The Ex-Im Bank reported that the wind turbines would be manufactured at its facility in Pennsylvania and generators would be supplied by ABB Power T&D Company (Bland, VA), blades by LM Glassfiber Inc. (Grand Forks, ND), and associated equipment and services from other U.S. suppliers.

[104] Export-Import Bank of the United States, "Ex-Im Approves $32.1 Million in Financing For Export of U.S. Wind Blades to Brazil ," press release, August 3, 2012, http://www.exim.gov/newsandevents/releases/2012/ex-im-approves-32-1-million-in-financing-for-export-of-u-s-wind-blades-to-brazil.cfm.

[105] KPMG International, *Taxes and Incentives for Renewable Energy*, June 2012, http://www.kpmg.com/Global/en/IssuesAndInsights/ArticlesPublications/Documents/taxes-incentives-renewable-energy-2012v3.pdf.

[106] Siemens, *Current Trends in Renewable Energy Markets*, p. 3, April 2012, http://www.iea.org/media/weowebsite/ebc/meetings/ebcmeeting-12-13june2012/SiemensTrendsinRenewableEnergyMarkets.pdf.

In Europe, feed-in tariffs[107] are among the policy tools that have been used to promote wind power, and have been credited by industry advocates like the European Wind Energy Association[108] with driving renewable energy growth, particularly in Denmark, Spain, and Germany. However, faced with a difficult fiscal and economic situation, some European countries have reduced their wind power feed-in tariffs and are taking a more critical look at their renewable energy policies.[109] For instance, in 2010, Spain announced it would reduce its wind subsidies by 35% from January 1, 2011, to January 1, 2013.[110] Some of the leading global wind turbine manufacturers, including Vestas and Gamesa, have downsized their operations to remain competitive, while others may place even more emphasis on exporting.

China's Renewable Energy Law, which took effect in 2006, is one measure that has driven growth in the domestic market.[111] China introduced a feed-in tariff for wind power generation in 2009.[112] The Chinese government also implemented various policies to encourage the development of local manufacturing and technology development.[113]

In the United States, various federal policies also have been instrumental in the development of a domestically based wind power sector, including:

- the production tax credit (PTC)/Investment Tax Credit (ITC), which will expire at the end of 2012;

- an advanced energy manufacturing tax credit (MTC), which reached its funding cap in 2010 (no additional funds were allocated to continue with the MTC);

- the Section 1603 Treasury Cash Grant Program, which required that wind projects begin construction by December 31, 2011, and be placed in service by December 31, 2012; and

---

[107] A feed-in tariff, or FIT, is a renewable energy policy that typically offers a guarantee of payments to project owners for the total amount of renewable energy they produce; access to the grid; and stable, long-term contracts (15-20 years). For more information see workshop presentation, Renewable Energy Feed-in Tariffs: An Analytical View, by Toby Couture, May 28, 2009. http://www.energy.ca.gov/2009_energypolicy/documents/2009-05-28_workshop/ presentations/01_Couture_Feed-in_Tariff_Wkshop_May_28_09.pdf.

[108] European Wind Energy Association, *Support Schemes for Renewable Energy, A Comparative Analysis of Payment Mechanisms in the EU*, 2002, p. 31, http://www.ewea.org/fileadmin/ewea_documents/documents/projects/rexpansion/ 050620_ewea_report.pdf.

[109] At least three studies have raised questions about the costs associated with Europe's support of its renewable energy sectors. A report by a Spanish academician, Dr. Gabriel Calzada, *Study of the Effects on Employment of Public Aid to Renewable Energy Sources*, argued that Spain's policies were an economic failure and cost many jobs. Another report by a Danish think tank, CEPOS, *Wind Energy: The Cost for Denmark*, also pointed to the costs of subsidizing Denmark's wind power industry. A third report by the German think tank, Rheinisch-Westfälisches Institut für Wirtschaftsforschung (RWI), *Economic Impacts from the Promotion of Renewable Energies: The German Experience*, argues that aid by the German government for wind power is now three times the cost of conventional electricity.

[110] Ben Backwell, "Subsidies to be Cut for Spain's Wind and Thermal Solar Sectors," *Recharge News*, July 5, 2010.

[111] For a detailed discussion of China's green energy policies, see CRS Report R41748, *China and the United States—A Comparison of Green Energy Programs and Policies*, by Richard J. Campbell

[112] GWEC, *Global Wind Report Annual Market Update 2010*, April 2011, pp. 30-33, http://www.gwec.net/index.php? id=180.

[113] Eric Martinot, *Renewable Power for China: Past, President and Future*, 2010, p. 6, http://www.martinot.info/ Martinot_FEP4_prepub.pdf.

- the Section 1705 Loan Guarantee Program for commercial projects, which includes manufacturing facilities that employ "new or significantly improved" technologies.

The wind industry asserts that a national renewable electricity standard is needed to create long-term stability and to attract investment in new turbine production facilities. **Table 5** provides an overview of selected federal programs affecting the U.S. wind power industry.

Table 5. Selected Energy Programs Affecting the U.S. Wind Industry

Program	Expiration Deadlines for Wind Generation/Manufacturing Projects
Production Tax Credit	December 31, 2012
Investment Tax Credit[a]	December 31, 2012
Advanced Manufacturing Tax Credit	Capped at $2.3 billion; 100% Allocated
1603 Cash Grant in Lieu of Tax Credit[b]	December 31, 2011 (begin construction) December 31, 2012 (placed in service)
1705 Loan Guarantee Program	September 30, 2011 (commence construction)
Bonus Depreciation Schedule	December 31, 2011, for 100% first-year bonus depreciation December 31, 2012, for 50% bonus

Source: Wind Energy Manufacturers Association, Supply Chain Issues from Tier 1 Suppliers and Component Makers, http://www.slideshare.net/LeslieFeen/supply-chain-issues-from-tier-1-suppliers-and-component-makers-wind-power-manufacturing-amp-supply-cha

a. The taxpayer who presumably is the owner of the relevant wind power project placed in service prior to December 31, 2012, can opt for a 30% ITC in lieu of the PTC. The 30% ITC for small commercial wind energy property extends through December 31, 2016.

b. The taxpayer owning the relevant wind power project can opt for a 30% cash grant from the U.S. Department of Treasury instead of a PTC, then select a one-time cash grant instead of tax credits.

Production Tax Credit (PTC)/Investment Tax Credit (ITC)

The PTC, the main policy tool in the deployment of U.S. wind power, was first adopted during the Administration of President George H. W. Bush as part of the Energy Policy Act of 1992 (P.L. 102-486). It has been a significant driver of the recent growth of the U.S. wind industry, but it is not a permanent part of the tax code and has lapsed on a number of occasions. In each of the years during which the PTC lapsed (2000, 2002, and 2004), meaning that it expired prior to being renewed, the level of additional deployed wind capacity slowed or collapsed when compared to the previous year's total: 93% in 2000, 73% in 2002, and 77% in 2004.[114] Yet, when the PTC incentive was extended in 2004, 2007, and 2009, the industry responded positively, increasing wind power capacity compared to the previous year. 2010 was an exception to this trend with a drop in wind capacity of nearly 50% from 2009, even with the PTC in place. In 2011, at 6,816 MW, annual installed wind capacity increased by 30% over the previous year. The annual cost of the PTC is estimated at about $1 billion a year.[115]

---

[114] AWEA, *Production Tax Credit*, What is the Production Tax Credit?, p. 1, http://www.awea.org/_cs_upload/issues/federal_policy/7785_1.pdf.

[115] U.S. Congress, House Committee on Science, Space, and Technology, Subcommittee on Investigations and (continued...)

Congress provided a three-year extension of the PTC through December 31, 2012, as part of the American Recovery and Reinvestment Act. The PTC provides an inflation-adjusted per kilowatt-hour (kWh) income tax benefit over the first 10 years of a wind project's operations, which in 2010 was 2.2 cents per kWh, and is a critical factor in financing new wind farms. In order to qualify, a wind farm must be completed and start generating power while the credit is in place, which would be by the end of 2012.[116] Wind project developers may elect to receive a 30% investment tax credit (IRC §48) in place of the PTC if the projects are placed in service prior to the end of 2012.[117]

AWEA advocates for a phase out of the PTC over six years, which it argues would encourage continued investment in the industry and would allow for extended growth of domestic turbine manufacturing.[118] The Governors' Wind Energy Coalition has called for a multi-year extension of the PTC of at least four years.[119] Given the uncertainty about the continuation of the PTC beyond 2012, along with the possible loss of other tax benefits, some in the industry have begun to refer to 2013 as "the valley of death"[120] in which industry support programs will end without any replacement policies.

Advanced Energy Manufacturing Tax Credit (MTC)

The Advanced Energy Manufacturing Tax Credit, also referred to as Section 48C of the Internal Revenue Code, was authorized in Section 1302 of the American Recovery and Reinvestment Act.[121] The MTC provided a 30% credit for companies for investments in new, expanded, or reequipped clean energy domestic manufacturing facilities built in the United States. Wind, solar panels, and electric vehicle batteries were among the 183 projects funded through the MTC before reaching its cap of $2.3 billion in 2010. The Obama Administration has requested another $5 billion for the 48C tax program. An extension of the MTC has been proposed through the Security in Energy and Manufacturing Act of 2011 (S. 591), or SEAM Act. It includes one

---

(...continued)

Oversight, *Impact of Tax Policies on the Commercial Application of Renewable Energy Technology*, 112th Cong., 2nd sess., April 19, 2012, p. 10, http://science.house.gov/sites/republicans.science.house.gov/files/documents/hearings/HHRG-112-SY21-WState-LLinowes-20120419.pdf.

[116] AWEA, *Production Tax Credit*, What is the Production Tax Credit?, p. 1, http://www.awea.org/_cs_upload/issues/federal_policy/7785_1.pdf.

[117] Internal Revenue Service Notice 2009-52, Election of Investment Tax Credit, Coordination with Department of Treasury Grants for Specified Energy Property in Lieu of Tax Credits, http://www.irs.gov/pub/irs-drop/n-09-52.pdf.

[118] In a December 12, 2012, letter to Congress, AWEA proposed a six-year reduction of the PTC between 2014 and 2018, with the tax credit starting at 100% of the current 2.2 cents a kilowatt-hour for projects started in 2013, followed by 90%, 80%, 70%, 60%, and then 60% of the current project level for projects placed in service from 2014 through 2018, with no PTC in 2019 or thereafter. AWEA, *Phase-Out of Wind Energy Production Tax Credit Would Enable U.S. Industry To Become Full Cost-Competitive*, December 12, 2012, http://www.awea.org/newsroom/pressreleases/Analysisonphaseout.cfm.

[119] Letter from Governor's Wind Energy Coalition to Congress, November 15, 2011, http://governorswindenergycoalition.org/wp-content/uploads/2011/03/GWC-PTC-Letter-Final2-11-15-11.pdfhttp://www.governorswindenergycoalition.org/assets/files/President Obama Wind Energy Letter %28July 24, 2011%29.pdf.

[120] Gloria Gonzalez, *U.S. Renewables Industry Searches for More Tax Breaks as Grants End*, Wind Energy Manufacturers Association , June 20, 2011, http://wema.membershipsoftware.org/blog_home.asp?Display=98.

[121] For more information see White House, *Fact Sheet: $2.3 Billion in New Clean Energy Manufacturing Tax Credits*, January 8, 2010, http://www.whitehouse.gov/the-press-office/fact-sheet-23-billion-new-clean-energy-manufacturing-tax-credits.

---

significant change from the original MTC; higher priority would be given to facilities that manufacture—rather than assemble—goods and components in the United States.[122]

Fifty-two wind manufacturing projects were awarded $364 million in tax credits under the MTC program.[123] Beneficiaries included many manufacturers that were already active, or that had announced that they intend to open new facilities, in the United States. Selected manufacturers of wind turbines, blades, towers, and gears that received tax credits under the 48C program are listed in **Appendix C**.

Other Wind-Related Programs

Tax benefits for wind projects include accelerated tax depreciation and bonus depreciation; the latter allowed wind farm owners to write off more than 50% of the capital costs of building a wind farm in 2008, 2009, and 2010. The 2010 Tax Act[124] increased the first-year bonus depreciation to 100% for new qualified property acquired and placed in service between September 8, 2010, and December 31, 2011, rather than 50% for the qualifying property. Bonus depreciation dropped to the lower 50% rate in 2012.[125]

Another ARRA incentive is a grant system administered by the U.S. Treasury Department. In lieu of tax credits, wind projects can receive a cash payment of up to 30% of the qualified capital costs. The Section 1603 Treasury cash grant program allows developers to opt for a cash payment instead of a tax break. To qualify, construction had to begin by December 31, 2011.[126] Wind projects under construction by year-end 2011 must be placed in service by December 31, 2012. Many in the wind industry credited the grants for keeping the sector healthy during the 2008 and 2009 recession.[127] A detailed discussion of the Section 1603 program can be found in CRS Report R41635, *ARRA Section 1603 Grants in Lieu of Tax Credits for Renewable Energy: Overview, Analysis, and Policy Options*, by Phillip Brown and Molly F. Sherlock.

The Section 1705 loan program, a temporary ARRA program administered by the Department of Energy, authorized loan guarantees for certain renewable energy projects, including wind projects. The program, which funded 26 projects, including four wind generation projects, expired on September 30, 2011. The combined wind commitments totaled $1.7 billion, or 9% of the $18.8 billion in 1705 program funding.[128] The Caithness Shepherds Flat wind generation

---

[122] "SEAM Act Will Build U.S. Wind Supply Chain Says Industry Group," *Industry Week*, May 12, 2010. http://www.industryweek.com/articles/seam_act__will_help_build_u-s-_wind_supply_chain_says_industry_group_21813.aspx?SectionID=2.

[123] White House, *The Recovery Act: Transforming the American Economy Through Innovation, Promoting Clean, Renewable Energy: Investments in Wind and Solar*, http://www.whitehouse.gov/recovery/innovations/clean-renewable-energy.

[124] The Tax Relief, Unemployment Insurance Reauthorization, and Job Creation Act of 2010 (P.L. 111-312) was signed by President Obama on December 17, 2010.

[125] Ryan Wiser and Mark Bolinger, *2011 Wind Technologies Market Report*, Lawrence Berkeley National Laboratory, August 2012, p. 57.

[126] Criteria for the start of construction are detailed in a U.S. Treasury guidance document, which can found on the Treasury Department's 1603 Grant Program website at http://www.treasury.gov/initiatives/recovery/Pages/1603.aspx.

[127] Mark Bolinger, Ryan Wiser, and Naim Darghouth, *Preliminary Evaluation of the Impact of the Section 1603 Treasury Grant Program on Renewable Energy Deployment in 2009*, Ernest Orlando Lawrence Berkeley National Laboratory, April 2010, p. ii, http://eetd.lbl.gov/ea/emp/reports/lbnl-3188e.pdf.

[128] Solar generation or solar manufacturing comprised the overwhelming majority (85%) of the 1705 loan guarantee (continued...)

---

project, said to be one of the largest onshore wind farms in the world, received a $1.3 billion loan.[129] GE manufactured the wind turbines. Loan guarantees were also extended to three other wind generation projects: Kahuku Wind Power, Granite Reliable, and Record Hill Wind. No wind turbine manufacturers were funded under the 1705 program.[130]

State Renewable Portfolio Standards

State renewable portfolio standards have encouraged the growth of the U.S. wind energy industry by requiring companies that sell electricity to retail customers to obtain a specified share of their electricity from renewable generation.[131] As of June 2012, mandatory RPS programs existed in 29 states and the District of Columbia.[132] The U.S. wind industry has long called for a national standard to increase investor confidence in the sector's long-term prospects. No such measure has passed Congress, although bills to establish national renewable standards have been passed by the Senate on three occasions and by the House of Representatives once.[133]

Conclusion

The expansion of the U.S. wind power manufacturing base will depend, at least in part, on government policy decisions. The production costs of U.S. plants that make turbine components appear to be competitive with those in other countries, and the difficulty and expense of transporting very bulky products over long distances serves as an obstacle to import competition.

Nonetheless, there are several obstacles that may impede the expansion of wind energy manufacturing in the United States. One is the history of policy-induced boom-and-bust cycles in wind energy investment, which may lead wind turbine manufacturers and component suppliers to conclude that future U.S. demand for their products is too uncertain. Another significant challenge affecting the sector's future is the availability of adequate transmission for power generated by wind farms. Most wind farms are located at a distance from the urban areas where most electricity is consumed, and a shortage of transmission capacity could hamper wind farm creation or expansion. Congress may wish to evaluate the seriousness of transmission issues in the context of other federal efforts to support wind generation.[134]

(...continued)

projects funded at $15.9 billion by the Department of Energy. A list of the 1705 Loan Program projects can be found at https://lpo.energy.gov/?page_id=45.

[129] Department of Energy, "DOE LPO Finalizes Deal on the World's Largest Wind Project to Date," press release, December 17, 2010, https://lpo.energy.gov/?p=1955.

[130] Nordic Windpower had received a conditional commitment of $16 million in 2009 for a wind turbine manufacturing project in Kansas City, MO, but abandoned its application in 2011. The company filed for Chapter 7 bankruptcy protection in October 2012.

[131] CRS Report R42576, *U.S. Renewable Electricity: How Does the Production Tax Credit (PTC) Impact Wind Markets?*, by Phillip Brown.

[132] U.S. Department of Energy, *2010 Wind Technologies Market Report*, August 2012, p. 58.

[133] See CRS Report R41493, *Options for a Federal Renewable Electricity Standard*, by Richard J. Campbell.

[134] CRS Report R42818, *U.S. Renewable Electricity: How Does Wind Generation Impact Competitive Power Markets?*, by Phillip Brown.

The structure of the wind manufacturing industry is also likely to undergo significant change. As is typical in budding industries, a large number of companies now compete in wind manufacturing. Mergers and failures are likely to lead to consolidation as the sector matures. As this report describes, competition in the wind turbine sector from new Asian entrants will likely become more significant in future years, but it is still unclear whether many of these companies have the technological abilities and financial resources to become significant players in the U.S. market.

Appendix A. Global Wind Turbine Manufacturers

Table A-1. Global Wind Turbine Manufacturers by Original Equipment Manufacturers (OEMs)

Top 10 by Annual Market Share (installed capacity), 2009, 2010, 2011

Manufacturer	Location of Headquarters	2009	Manufacturer	Location of Headquarters	2010	Manufacturer	Location of Headquarters	2011
Vestas	Denmark	12.50%	Vestas	Denmark	14.80%	Vestas	Denmark	12.90%
GE	U.S.	12.4	Sinovel	China	11.1	Goldwind	China	9.4
Sinovel	China	9.2	GE	U.S.	9.6	GE	U.S.	8.8
Enercon	Germany	8.5	Goldwind	China	9.5	Gamesa	Spain	8.2
Goldwind	China	7.2	Enercon	Germany	7.2	Enercon	Germany	7.9
Gamesa	Spain	6.7	Suzlon	India	6.9	Suzlon	India	7.7
Dongfang	China	6.5	Dongfang	China	6.7	Sinovel	China	7.3
Suzlon	India	6.4	Gamesa	Spain	6.6	Guodian United Power	China	7.1
Siemens	Germany	5.9	Siemens	Germany	5.9	Siemens	Germany	6.3
Repower	Germany	3.4	United Power	China	4.2	MingYang WindPower	China	2.9

Sources: *Vestas Remains Top Wind Turbine Maker, Goldwind Is Second, BTM Consult*, March 26, 2012.

Notes: Market share data is reported in MW terms and is based on installations in the year in question, not on turbine shipments or orders.

Appendix B. Selected Examples of U.S. Wind Turbine Production Facilities

Table B-1. Examples: U.S. Turbine Production Facilities

Wind Turbine Manufacturer/Headquarters	U.S. Location	Wind Turbine Production Facilities
Gamesa (Spain)	PA	Gamesa, the first foreign-based wind turbine manufacturer to set up full production facilities in the United States, opened a plant at a former U.S. Steel factory in Ebensburg, PA, in 2005. Gamesa also operates a nacelle manufacturing plant in Fairless Hills, PA. It invested over $175 million in these plants and received $15 million in state subsidies and tax credits. In 2012, Gamesa reduced its workforce at the two plants by 160 workers, citing lower demand and the possible expiration of the production tax credit.[a]
Suzlon (India)	MN	Suzlon opened a rotor blade manufacturing facility in Pipestone, MN, in 2006, with an investment of $8.5 million, its first manufacturing facility outside India. That factory, which once employed over 500 workers, was idled in 2010 save for blade repair and customer service operations, and most of its workers have been laid off.[b] Suzlon acquired the German manufacturer REpower in March 2012.
Siemens (Germany)	IA/KN	Siemens opened a wind turbine blade factory in Fort Madison, IA in 2007 and a nacelle factory in Hutchinson, KS in 2010. In 2012, Siemens announced a reduction of its U.S. wind power workforce by more than 37%, citing low natural-gas prices, a slow economic recovery, and the possible expiration of the PTC.[c]
Vestas (Denmark)	CO	Vestas opened a blade production plant in Windsor, CO, and an R&D center in Louisville, CO in 2010 and another blade manufacturing plant in Brighton, CO in 2012. Vestas received an incentive package of approximately $4 million to invest in Colorado, including grants, tax rebates, and job-training funds. In 2012, employment at Vestas's factories in Colorado fell to 1,200 from more than 1,700 at the start of the year.[d]
Nordex (Germany)	AR	Nordex opened a nacelle assembly plant in 2010, which represented a $40 million investment. It expected to open a blade manufacturing plant in 2012 in Jonesboro, AR, but those plans have yet to be realized.
Mitsubishi (Japan)	AR	Mitsubishi in 2012 announced that it would indefinitely delay the opening of its nacelle assembly facility in Fort Smith, AR. The company had stated that the facility would employ 400 workers.[e]

Source: Compiled by CRS from various sources including company annual reports, press releases, news reports, and information from AWEA.

a. *Business News in Brief*, July 6, 2012, Philadelphia Inquirer, http://articles.philly.com/2012-07-06/business/32566874_1_wind-turbines-reports-passenger-refinery.

b. David Shaffer, *Pipestone Wind-Turbine Factory Idled; 110 Layoffs*, StarTribune, November 1, 2010, http://www.startribune.com/business/106490454.html?refer=y.

c. Laura DiMugno, *More PTC Fallout: Siemens Cuts 37% of its U.S. Wind Energy Workforce*, North American WindPower, September 18, 2012, http://nawindpower.com/e107_plugins/content/content.php?content.10418#.UMZJnXe3qVk.

d. *Vestas Statement on Colorado Layoffs*, Denver Business Journal, October 11, 2012, http://www.bizjournals.com/denver/news/2012/10/11/vestas-statement-on-colorado-layoffs.html?page=all.

e. Rusty Garrett, *Mitsubishi Mothballs Fort Smith Wind Turbine Plant*, Times Record, April 2, 2012, http://swtimes.com/sections/news/mitsubishi-%E2%80%9Cmothballs%E2%80%9D-fort-smith-wind-turbine-plant.html.

Appendix C. 48C Manufacturing Tax Credit

Table C-1. Selected Wind Manufacturers Receiving Section 48C Manufacturing Tax Credit

Applicant	Tax Credit Requested	State
Siemens	$28,328,379	IL
Nordex	$22,153,500	AR
Merrill Technologies Group	$22,021,500	MI
Vestas	$21,600,000	CO
Vestas	$21,589,200	CO
Tindall Corporation	$16,750,500	SC
Winergy	$12,786,000	IL
Brevini	$12,750,000	IN
Vela Gear Systems	$11,604,440	MI
Vestas	$8,580,600	CO
Hexcel Corporation	$8,139,510	CO
TPI Composites	$5,135,241	NE
Mitsubishi Power Systems	$5,100,000	AR
Siemens	$4,331,700	KS
TPI Composites	$3,902,921	IA
Siemens	$3,450,900	IA
Nordic Windpower	$3,000,000	ID
Alstom	$2,725,800	TX

Source: Strategic Partnerships, Inc. http://www.spartnerships.com/reports/ARRA%20Energy%20Manufacturing%20Tax%20Credit%20Awards.pdf.

Notes: A tax credit is a "dollar for dollar" reduction in tax liability. As an example, if a manufacturer earns $10 million and owes $3.5 million in taxes, then a $1 million tax credit would reduce the company's tax liability from $3.5 million to $2.5 million.

Author Contact Information

Michaela D. Platzer
Specialist in Industrial Organization and Business
mplatzer@crs.loc.gov, 7-5037

Acknowledgments

Thanks to Amber Wilhelm for contributing the graphics to this report.